The Internet for the
TYPEWRITER
Generation™

The Internet for the
TYPEWRITER
Generation™

Daniel J. Fingerman

TEN SPEED PRESS

Ten Speed Press
P.O. Box 7123
Berkeley, California 94707
www.tenspeed.com

Distributed in Australia by Simon and Schuster Australia, in Canada by Ten Speed Press Canada, in New Zealand by Tandem Press, in South Africa by Real Books, and in the United Kingdom and Europe by Airlift Books.

Cover design by Catherine Jacobes
Cover photography © PhotoDisc
Interior design by Chris Hall

Library of Congress Cataloging-in-Publication Data on file with the publisher.

First printing, 1999
Printed in Canada

1 2 3 4 5 6 7 8 9 10 — 03 02 01 00 99

Publisher's Note: The accuracy and completeness of the information provided herein and the opinions stated herein are not guaranteed or warranted to produce any particular results, and the advice and strategies contained herein may not be suitable for every individual.

Contents

Acknowledgments

While writing *The Internet for the Typewriter Generation* I had the good fortune to collaborate with a number of very skillful individuals.

Thanks go out to Phil Wood, publisher of Ten Speed Press, and self-avowed computer curmudgeon. I will be most delighted (and moderately astonished) if this book motivates him to see the error of his ways and to begin exploring the Internet.

Jason Rath, project editor, put in innumerable hours encouraging, cajoling, and otherwise moving this book to completion. He and Joli Bennett helped me polish my words to the level of sheen displayed in the following pages.

Mary Bitondo performed admirably (and quickly), scanning the manuscript for technical accuracy and completeness.

Jerry Fingerman served as an excellent prototype of an Internet novice, letting me know what sections of the manuscript made sense and, frequently, which didn't. Big brothers are like that.

Special thanks to Theo Jolosky for help, ideas, and support, not only on this book, but ever since Fern Hill.

Major thanks go to tens of millions of unnamed people around the world who so freely share their knowledge and expertise on millions of websites on the Internet. They—and we—make the Internet what it is.

Finally, and certainly the most important contributors to this work, are Lynne, Kevin, Beth, my extended family, and friends, without whose love and support this all would have been impossible.

Introduction

The phone rang at around six o'clock in the evening. It was Dr. R.K., my wife's gynecologist. We were expecting the call. The biopsy had been the day before. My wife and I both got on the phone and the doctor delivered the news: "infiltrating ductal carcinoma," the most common form of breast cancer.

The date was February 22, 1996. This book was born in the early-morning hours of the following day. Eventually, my wife managed to fall asleep that night, but I was wide-awake at 2:00 A.M., my mind racing with worries and questions—so many unknowns. I decided to go see if I could find some information on breast cancer on the Internet.

Over the next few hours, I discovered literally thousands of pages of information on the topic that suddenly loomed so large in our lives. In subsequent months, my wife and I received guidance, advice, and support from people we met on the Internet who had been down the path ahead of us and who were willing to share their experiences. Their frequent e-mails gave us both information and encouragement.

This was my first serious search for information on the Internet, though I had dabbled in the Internet for years. I quickly learned that the Internet—that vague, diffuse "newfangled" entity that exists in something called "cyberspace"—is a virtually unlimited source of information.

Since my wife's surgery, subsequent therapy and recovery, our lives have returned to near normal. We raise our kids, work, go shopping, travel, think about investments, wonder where to go to dinner Saturday night, stay in touch with friends and relatives, and decide if we should go to this movie or that one. We frequently tap the Internet for each of these tasks.

This is a pragmatic book to introduce you to the Internet. The book is de-

signed to help you learn to explore the Internet in your own way, at your own pace, as your needs and interests dictate. You will learn to use tools that will aid you in your exploration, no matter what your experience with computers.

The Internet for the Typewriter Generation will teach you just enough to put the Internet to work for you—enabling you to look up movie reviews, find the latest medical information, send e-mail to relatives living across town or around the world, and much more. As you discover more about what you can do on the Internet, I expect that you will move from "I didn't know I could do that!" to "I wonder if I can . . . ?" A world of information and connection with others is at your fingertips.

Good luck. Enjoy your journey.

Chapter 1

What Is This Internet Thing Anyway, and Why Would I Want To Investigate It?

For the times they are a-changin'.
Bob Dylan

Especially now, the times are a-changin', and at an increasingly rapid rate. Amid all of the changes taking place around us sits a remarkable new tool, the Internet, a tool that moves us into a new era—the era of information.

Over the Internet, information on virtually any topic is immediately available on your computer. Whatever your interests, whatever your needs, there is information on the Internet that can help you solve an immediate problem, learn new information, or enjoy life more.

Isn't It Difficult To Learn To Use the Internet?

Consider an analogy. Do you personally have the skills necessary to bring electricity into a new house from power lines outside? Can you run the wires, install the circuit breakers, or attach light fixtures and wall switches? Relatively few people reading this have those specialized skills.

Yet, you use electricity all day long. Without thinking twice, you turn on and off the lights, television, radio, microwave oven, and electric toothbrush. Although you may not know how to deal directly with electricity (nor perhaps even how it works!) all of these devices are tools that allow you to tap the power of electricity.

The Internet is much like electricity. Do you need to know how to string wiring to use the Internet? Not at all. Do you need to know how the Internet works? Again, no. All you need to know are the Internet equivalents to the light

switch on the wall or the microwave oven controls. In almost all ways, using the Internet is simpler than that most daunting of all household high-tech tasks: setting the clock on the VCR.

This book is designed to show you how simple it is to use existing tools, which ease your entry onto the Internet and allow you to find information of interest and use to you.

Old Dogs *Can* Learn New Tricks

This "Internet" is an entirely new realm that did not exist when most of us were growing up. Nor did color television, FM radio, push-button telephones, ATMs, or voice mail. Yet, most of us now consider these devices just another part of our technological landscape. We use them without thinking twice, albeit sometimes grudgingly.

I mention this to remind you that in the last decade or two you have continued to learn to use new technologies. You learn the technology when it becomes valuable to you. Soon you will begin to see how valuable the Internet can be to *you*. Just as with your television, telephone, and ATM, you will be able to master the little bit of technology necessary for you to use the Internet. You need to learn only a very few skills to begin to explore its capabilities. The more you explore, the more you will discover regarding new ways in which to interact with the Internet. New skills will very likely come to you over time in a totally natural manner.

The Internet has developed a mystique around it. There is an image that it is some mysterious, extraordinarily technical entity, inaccessible to any but the most technologically sophisticated individuals. The mystique is a lie. The Internet is extremely accessible to anyone who has a computer and a curiosity. Yes, old dogs can learn new tricks.

What's in This Book?

Remember Joe Friday's most famous line in *Dragnet:* "Just the facts, Ma'am"? That is what this book provides—just the facts: the bare essentials necessary to get you up and running and exploring the Internet on your own.

Before I decided to write this book, I researched the existing Internet-related books. There were (and are) literally thousands of books available that explore this or that aspect of the Internet. Yet, not one book I could find was designed for readers who had little familiarity with personal computers—those of us from the typewriter generation. That is why this book explains the Internet using language that everyone can understand, even people new to computers.

This book will be as short on jargon as possible. It will be long on analogies, wherever they are appropriate. If you are about to interact with personal computers for the first time, I will recommend you locate someone who can help you get your computer up and running. At first, there is no real need for you to learn to do so. Later, maybe. But worry about later, later.

What Will I Learn?

Think back to when you first learned to drive a car. Perhaps it had a standard transmission. You certainly did not begin to learn to drive it by tackling the hills of San Francisco. You first learned what each of those pedals on the floor were for, when to push each one in, how far to push, and how quickly to release it. You practiced those skills for some time. You first drove on flat ground with no one around. Slowly you learned to handle small hills, and finally you could tackle the hills of San Francisco or Hong Kong.

This book will teach you the Internet analogs to the pedals in your car. You will drive in flat Internet "parking lots" until you have learned and are comfortable with the skills.

In short, this book will help you master the basics.

What Could I Do on the Internet—If I Were Willing to Try?

Consider some brief scenarios that illustrate why you might want to begin to explore the Internet.

Reconnect with Old Friends

One day last year I received the following message in my e-mail:

> Surprise and hello! (Caveat: If this is some other Dan Fingerman, not the Minneapolis-MIT-old friend person, apologies and an embarrassed smile...)
> I've been wondering where you've been and what you've been up to and

have tried unsuccessfully to find you on e-mail a couple of times, on the assumption that you, of all people, would be "wired." I recently found out about **whowhere!*** *and here you are (or not . . . see caveat, above).*

If this is the real you, then hello from the real me...still in Toronto, now teaching at _____ University, and other family and professional stuff which I'll fill you in on once we establish contact. Looking forward to hearing from you!

Judy L.

Judy and I grew up near one another in Minneapolis. We dated a bit during high school and college. We enjoyed one another's company, but after we each got married, we went our separate ways. She ended up in Toronto, while I settled near San Francisco. We lost touch.

After about twenty-five years of no communication, out of the blue came this e-mail from my old friend. Coincidentally, it arrived only a few weeks before I was going to Toronto on a business trip. While I was there, I went to dinner at her home, where I met her delightful family and generally caught up on a few decades apart. We now stay in touch by e-mail every few months, sharing family milestones or an occasional joke. In an e-mail sent after our dinner together, Judy wrote:

This is one of the reasons I love the Internet. People who think it is impersonal are missing the point!

I couldn't agree more.

Do you have friends from long ago about whom you wonder from time to time? Would it be interesting to find them and reconnect?

The Internet gives you a variety of tools for doing just that.

Send Information

In 1860, the Pony Express transported mail from St. Joseph, Missouri, to San Francisco in only ten days, about half the time it had taken to send mail via

---

*An Internet tool that will be discussed in Chapter 4.

stagecoach. With the arrival of the Postal Service, a letter could travel from coast to coast faster than ever before. Today, using a fax machine or a computer, you can send a mail message, including photographs if you like, across the street, across the country, or halfway around the world, virtually instantaneously.

Do you have friends or relatives who live in another state or country? Perhaps you have children or grandchildren in college with whom you would like to maintain regular contact. You know they probably will write you letters only rarely, might call now and then, yet they may well respond to a "hi, how are you?" e-mail moments after you send it.

Most people who have grown up using personal computers and the Internet think no more of receiving and responding to an e-mail message than you and I might think of picking up the telephone and calling someone. It's second nature. When making a phone call, if the line is busy or there is no answer, we hang up and may or may not place the call later. The e-mail message, in contrast, awaits the recipient.

The Internet gives you a tool for establishing and maintaining frequent contact with friends and loved ones, no matter how great the distance.

Have Conversations Without Using the Telephone

You may have seen ads for America Online, often referred to as "AOL." It is a company that, as you will see in the following chapters, is central to Internet access. It has implemented a wonderful messaging technology, called AOL Instant Messenger, or AIM.

Using this technology, I can be informed whenever my son is on the Internet in his college dorm room, when an old Peace Corps friend is online (i.e., connected to the Internet) in his office in Johor Bahru, Malaysia, or when my brother is on the Internet in his den in Minneapolis. Similarly, they can be informed of my online status. When two of us are connected to the Internet at the same time, either of us can initiate a private "chat" with the other. (Or I can preserve my privacy by declining to let others know when I am online. Such privacy issues are covered in later chapters.)

For example, over the months that I sat at my desk writing this book, frequently a box would appear on my screen containing the words "Hi, Dad." My

son was in his dorm room and saw on his computer that I was on the Internet. He took the opportunity to pop into my life to say hello. I would type a response to him, he would respond to me, and we would type back and forth for a minute or two, or perhaps for half an hour. We would discuss everything from the weather to his weekend outings in New York. From time to time we would also commiserate on our apparent genetic inclination to procrastinate our writing projects—him with his term papers and me with my book! AIM continues to give us a quick and easy way to "check in" with each other.

You might ask, "What's the big deal? I can do the same thing with a telephone call. Besides, then I can just talk, not have to type." Of course, you are right. However, how often do you call friends and family scattered around the city, the country, or the world? Instant Messaging* allows you to make spontaneous connections. Better yet, AIM is free if you are on the Internet, unlike long-distance telephone calls.

IMing is discussed further in Chapter 6 of this book.

Get Information on a Topic of Interest

Recently, I joined a small group of friends for dinner one evening. At that dinner, I met a faculty member from a university in Krasnoyarsk, Siberia, who was attending a workshop at the University of California, Berkeley. Over the course of the evening, I learned an enormous amount about Krasnoyarsk, my friend's university, and Siberian politics.

I was curious to learn more. I decided to look on the Internet to see if I could find out anything more about Krasnoyarsk.

Within two minutes, I knew the population of Krasnoyarsk (over three million) and how that population was distributed throughout the geographic region. I found out that the average January temperature in part of the region is -33°F. I learned about the local terrain (flood plain along the Yenesei River rising to the mid-Siberian plateau) and about local flora and fauna (450 species of plants, 342 species of birds, and 89 species of mammals).

Did I need to know any of this? Of course not. But I was curious, and the Internet provided me with the tools to satisfy my curiosity.

*Instant Messaging is often called "IMing" (pronounced "eye-em-ing") as in "I'm IMing Kevin right now."

Are there topics that have always interested you, about which you would like to know more? Hobbies? History? Recipes? Nostalgia?

The Internet gives you the tools to research all of these.

Receive Travel Advice

Last year, my wife, daughter, and I were going to be spending a few days in Paris on vacation. We wanted recommendations for an interesting, small hotel somewhere in the central city area. One night I posted a note on the Internet equivalent to the "community service" bulletin board of your local super-market. This Internet bulletin board was devoted specifically to travel in France. In the note I posed my question and indicated the general area we wanted to stay. By the next morning, I had received five separate recommendations of hotels, inns, and bed and breakfasts, in and around Paris. We also received tips on restaurants, "must-see" museums, and suggestions on how best to get from the airport to the central city. It worked for Paris; the same holds true for Peoria.

The Internet gives you not only a portal to information, but also access to expertise from people all around the world who are willing to share ideas with you. What's more, this sort of information is easy to learn to access, even if you are a computer novice.

For example, during Family Weekend at my son's college, I attended an event in the library. There I happened to strike up a conversation with another family visiting the campus. They live in a metropolitan area on the East Coast, and both parents were self-proclaimed Internet novices.

When they found out that I live near San Francisco, they asked what I knew about lodging for a ski vacation they were planning at Lake Tahoe. Since we were in the campus library, my immediate reaction was to check on the Internet. We headed to a public Internet terminal, and within two minutes I had printed out information, including photographs, of three or four different homes they could rent in the Tahoe area.

Two weeks later I received an e-mail from the father:

Meeting you [on campus] has already been of great help to us as it gave us the idea of using the Internet to plan our trip. Our travel agent booked us

into a resort of some sort and my family rebelled. They said, "We just want a cabin in the woods."

Believe it or not, at your instigation, I got on the net and within a few hours had found us a number of "cabins in the woods" and we all had looked at photos of several before choosing one! Now all we have to do is wait until February.

The Internet gave him, as it gives you, ready access to this type of information.

Track Your Investments

Are you a market watcher? Do you like to track your investment portfolio? You can get stock quotes and up-to-the-minute news on companies of interest to you. Be notified by e-mail when news occurs that concerns a company of interest to you. Trade stocks over the Internet inexpensively, saving brokers' commissions.

The Internet gives you the ability to do all of this easily and conveniently.

Find the Most Current Medical Information

If you or a loved one is diagnosed with virtually any medical condition, you can find a wide variety of useful information on the Internet. You can begin your education about the condition with brochures or reports published in the mass media. Find information on treatment options. Learn about the latest research and experimental drugs. Correspond with others who have the condition, as well as with those who love and support them. Discuss long-term implications of the condition. Learn from those who have "been there."

The Internet gives you immediate access to all of these connections.

Find Out the Latest News, Weather, Sports

If you're the type of person who can't wait to get the latest news or sports scores, the Internet plugs you in to what's happening virtually as soon as it happens. Tap into CNN, Associated Press, UPI, Reuters, ESPN, and foreign news agencies as fast as the television and radio networks do.

Would you like to find out the latest jai alai results? Are you interested in the latest collegiate volleyball scores? Would you like to voice your opinion on the current "bad guys" in professional wrestling or discover who's who in professional bowling?

Could it be useful for you to see the weather forecast for when you get off the plane tomorrow in Memphis? Or Madrid? Or Melbourne? Should you take your golf clubs or your snowshoes?

The Internet gives you the tools to access all of this information, virtually instantly.

What Equipment Do I Need?

The next chapter details the initial steps for using the Internet. For now, all you need to know is that three general components are required:

- A computer, in some form or other. Maybe it will look the way you envision a computer looking. Maybe it will look more like a small three-ring binder, which is called a "laptop" computer. Maybe it will look like the television set in the corner of your living room. In fact, maybe it *will be* the television set in the corner of your living room.

- A way to hook up the computer to the outside world. Usually you will use a telephone line to which your computer is connected. Alternatively, it could be via your cable TV connection.

- A program that, in effect, interprets what you tell it to do and sends that information out onto the Internet. Subsequently, it receives the electronic information from the Internet and feeds it back to your computer in a form you can use. This program is called a "browser."

Isn't This All Expensive?

Not necessarily. Many, if not most, community libraries have computers you can use to access the Internet for free. Many churches and synagogues have computers available for their congregants' use. Perhaps you can begin your Internet exploration at your neighbor's computer or at the community center.

Another option is to ask around at your next family get-together. See if anyone has a computer they are no longer using that they would be willing to lend to you. For initial exploration of the Internet, a two- or three-year-old computer is generally fine. Tell your relatives what you want the computer for, and chances are good that someone will be willing to set you up with an adequate system.

If cost is not an issue for you, or if you are otherwise stymied in your quest for a computer, you can always purchase a computer for your home. Prices continue to tumble for personal computers. Currently, you can purchase a home computer that is excellent for Internet use for under $1,000. Alas, my crystal ball is too foggy to allow me to predict how low prices will fall in the future. But they will fall.

If you choose to purchase a computer, you should recruit a computer-literate friend to assist you in the process. Explain to that person exactly what you want to use your computer for. Emphasize that it does not need to be state-of-the-art, nor even close to it. You just need a system adequate for Internet browsing. If you do not know exactly what you are looking for, *don't* just walk into the local computer megastore and depend on a sales clerk's advice. Many clerks may listen carefully to your needs and recommend an appropriate system that is within your budget. However, there is a tendency in the computer world to assume that bigger, more, and faster is inherently better. It's also more expensive. Smaller, less, and slower (and lower priced) may be just fine for your needs.

This is covered in more detail in Chapter 2.

A Word of Reassurance

As you begin to explore the Internet, rest assured that you cannot break anything—neither on your computer nor on any other one—by pushing any button on your computer or by clicking on anything on the screen. So don't worry. You cannot do anything wrong. You may not always accomplish what you set out to do, but you cannot do anything irrevocable. Relax and enjoy yourself!

What's Next?

The Internet is an amazing new frontier offering information, enjoyment, connections, and wisdom. There is also a lot of nonsense, rubbish, and obscenity on it. In a sense, the Internet simply reflects society.

Once you acquire the tools to explore the Internet, it will be up to you to seek out and take advantage of those areas that are valuable to you.

It is a wonderful and exciting challenge to do so.

Chapter 2

Gadgetry You Will Need

The Internet is a computer-based medium. You may have heard the term "World Wide Web" or "the Information Superhighway" used to describe it. Indeed, the Internet can be thought of as a web of computer systems that do, indeed, stretch around the world. Your computer can communicate with your friend's computer, or with one belonging to General Motors, General Electric, and many others.

The fact that the Internet is a collection of computers that are linked together is only of secondary importance to you and me. More important to us is how we get connected to that network. This chapter discusses what gadgetry we'll need to get where we want to go.

In order to browse the Internet, you will need to have access to a computer of some sort, together with a few accessories. The table to the right lists some of the common terms used to describe this equipment.

Do I Really Need To Buy a Computer?

Perhaps not. Before you order a computer from your local computer emporium or from an infomercial you saw on channel 62 at 2:00 A.M., consider these options:

- Call the local library, community college, museum, community center, or a nearby church or synagogue to see if they have computers available for community members to use.

Jargon

Hardware
> The physical gadgetry you need to hook up to the Internet. Includes such items as a computer, modem, and a phone line.

Modem
> A device that attaches to (or is inside) your computer and allows you to connect your computer to a telephone line.

Browsers
> Specific programs (or "software") used to explore the Internet. The two major browsers currently available are Netscape Navigator and Microsoft Internet Explorer. America Online also has its own browser.

WebTV
> This service allows you to hook your television up to the Internet, using your home telephone line. If you use WebTV, you don't need to have a separate computer.

• See if your friends or relatives know of anyone who has a computer you can borrow to begin your Internet investigation. Chances are good that if you tell them you want to explore the Internet and stay in closer touch using e-mail, they'll be delighted to help you find one.

There are many advantages to accessing the Internet in one of these ways. For one, you can get up and running on the Internet quickly and inexpensively. If you use a computer at the local library or similar facility, chances are good you'll have advisors available should you need guidance or encounter something confusing on the screen. If you take a "hand-me-down" computer, you may have its previous owner as an on-call consultant, at least until you get up and running on your own (or until you wear out your "call me any time" welcome!).

There are, however, some advantages to getting a new computer. If you purchase or lease a new computer, you can pretty much be assured of receiving brand new equipment, all of which was working properly when it left the manufacturer. You can be reasonably sure that it will work as advertised, allowing you to access the Internet as easily as possible. Also, should your computer stop working, for whatever reason, you will likely have a warranty that will cover the cost of repairing your equipment.

The Best Advice You Will Read in This Book

As you begin investigating this new realm of computers and the Internet, find yourself a computer buddy/tutor/mentor.

Whether you buy a new computer or use someone else's, a knowledgeable guide can be invaluable. Ask around. Maybe this person will be a neighbor your age who has been on the Internet for the last few years. Maybe it will be the relative who loaned you the computer. Perhaps it will be someone you know from church or a community group. Maybe it will be the fifteen-year-old across the street to whom you could pay a modest fee for assistance in setting up your system and getting your Internet connection up and running.

In many ways the last option is the best. If you commit to paying a young person for assistance, you may be more inclined to call on him or her when you need help. If you are relying on the kindness of a neighbor or relative, you may be more hesitant to impose on their freely given time.

Incidentally, you should realize that you would not be alone in adopting this strategy. The *New York Times* reported last year that for the week between Christmas and New Year's, the video game system producer Nintendo of America hired 150 high school students to serve as "play counselors," staffing telephone help lines to assist customers in hooking up their new game systems.

One of the temporary workers, a high school senior quoted in the article, was asked why he and his friends have no difficulty hooking up a VCR or Nintendo game system. "Maybe it's the way society brought us up," he replied. "Or maybe we're just more, you know, advanced."

Why fight it? Just find yourself a computer helper who just might be more, you know, advanced.

What Kind of Computer Do I Need?

Computer technology changes fast, faster than virtually any other technology now in existence. At a computer trade show, Microsoft chairman Bill Gates reportedly said, "If GM had kept up with technology like the computer industry has, we would all be driving twenty-five-dollar cars that got a thousand miles to the gallon."

My rule of thumb is that whenever I purchase a new computer, I assume it is obsolete by the time I get it out of the box. Even though my new computers tend to be "top of the line" when I purchase them, by the time I have a new system up and running, the "top of the line" has gone up a few notches.

If you are intending to purchase a new computer, you should be familiar with a few terms and numbers:

Term	What is it?	Names and numbers you should look for
CPU	The <u>C</u>entral <u>P</u>rocessing <u>U</u>nit is the gadget that actually does the computing. The numbers attached to the CPU indicate how fast it is. Bigger numbers are better.	If you are buying an IBM-compatible computer, get a 486 (minimum), Pentium II, or Celeron CPU. The new system should have a CPU speed of 133 megahertz (MHz) as an absolute *minimum*. (You probably won't be able to find one that slow unless someone is lending or giving it to you.) More common are speeds of 300MHz to 550MHz. Faster CPUs are always on the horizon. The newest Apple Macintosh models are called Power Macintosh G3. The name of the CPU is Power PC G3. Its speeds are up to 400MHz (266, 300, 350). Other models suitable to Internet access: iMac, PowerMac 601, 603, 604, Quadra, and Centris series.
RAM	<u>R</u>andom <u>A</u>ccess <u>M</u>emory is the work area in your computer. As you type your word-processing documents, your words are held in RAM until you save them on your hard drive (see below). RAM is measured in "megabytes" (MB). For information on megabytes, see below.	To be at least moderately efficient on the Internet, your computer should have *at least* 16MB of RAM. 32MB is better, 64MB or more, better still. You can get away with 16MB, though some processes might be slow or even impossible to perform. On most Apple Macintosh computers, RAM is 64MB or more.

Term	What is it?	Names and numbers you should look for
Modem	The device that connects your computer to the telephone line.	The minimum modem speed you should get is 28.8K. More common are 56K modems.
CD-ROM	A specialized compact disc player for your computer. Among other things, it allows you to load new programs into your computer.	24X or higher. The higher the number, the higher the rate of transfer of information. While you need a CD-ROM, I don't consider its speed to be crucial. What we're really talking about here is a device that might take 10, rather than 5 seconds to do whatever it does. One of my old computers has a 2X CD-ROM. Suppose it takes me two minutes to perform some task. If it were a 40X CD-ROM, it would take me about six seconds total. I perform such tasks perhaps once every couple of months. Two minutes wasted in two months: personally, I can live with that.
Hard Drive	This is the giant filing cabinet built into your computer, where you permanently store information. It is measured in units of "bytes." (See below for information on "bytes.") This storage is relatively inexpensive.	New computers have hard drives 3GB (gigabytes) and larger. It's amazing how hard drive space fills up. It's convenient to have hard drives of 2GB to 10GB on new systems.

As mentioned above, information storage space in your computer is measured in terms of "bytes." You might find it interesting to get a little perspective on the quantities we are discussing. The following table should help you better understand what these terms mean.

The smallest unit of information is	1 byte	Think of one byte as one letter or number or space, the sort of information you find on one Scrabble tile.
1,000 bytes make up a	Kilobyte (KB)	One typed, double spaced page contains about one kilobyte of information.
1,000 kilobytes make up a	Megabyte (MB)	A short novel contains about a megabyte of information. The complete works of Shakespeare can be contained in roughly five megabytes of storage space.
1,000 megabytes make up a	Gigabyte (GB)	Thirty linear shelf feet of encyclopedias contain about one gigabyte of information.

What Is WebTV?

WebTV gives you another alternative to buying a computer. Sony, Mitsubishi, Philips, and other manufacturers have collaborated with WebTV to create a VCR-like box containing a *de facto* computer that connects to your television and phone line. You can then explore the Internet and send and receive e-mail from the comfort of your sofa. You can enter information with a wireless remote control device or with an optional keyboard.

The advantages of WebTV are that you use a familiar device to explore unfamiliar territory—the Internet—and that it is easy to get set up and running. To set it up, you plug one end of a cord into your TV, VCR, or cable box, and the other end into a phone jack. You then follow simple directions to program the remote control to work with your TV and VCR or cable box. Finally, you turn on your TV, register for the service, and off you go!

In an article on the front page of the business section of the *San Francisco Chronicle*, a seventy-three-year-old WebTV user in New Jersey extolled its virtues:

> *She fears the personal computer—"I'm very intimidated by it," she said— but her son . . . bought her a WebTV and it has proved perfect to keep in touch with grandchildren at college and friends who've moved to the Sun Belt.*
>
> *"It's marvelous for e-mail," she said. "It's easier than the telephone, where you can't get through or they're not in. This way, they get the message quickly."*

How Do I Choose—Computer or WebTV?

As with all things in life, there are pluses and minuses on both sides. The **advantages** of using a personal computer over WebTV for accessing the Internet include:

- Speed. You may tend to see information on your screen faster, especially if you purchase a new computer with a fast modem.

- Larger storage capacity for information you find on the Internet that you might want to keep accessible for future reference.

- Ability to use the computer for purposes other than investigating the Internet.

- Availability of hand-me-down computers from friends or relatives.

- Opportunity to impress your friends with your new, hi-tech toy!

Disadvantages of a personal computer:

- Investment. At this time a new computer will cost approximately $700 to $3,000. A basic WebTV system is around $200.

- Space. Your TV is probably already comfortably settled into your house. You need to make space in which to set up a new personal computer.

Which option do you choose? Your decision will probably be based on budget considerations, space availability in your house, advice of friends, and access to other Internet computers.

What Else Do I Need?

The gadgetry described earlier is generally referred to as "hardware." The pieces collectively make up the physical components that are referred to as the "computer."

By way of analogy, you might think of the hardware as roughly equivalent to the devices that make up your automobile: the steering wheel, tires, spark plugs, and so on. Of course, having a car is only useful if you fill its fuel tank with gas. The gas in your car is equivalent to the software (also called "programs") on your computer. The fanciest computer available would be useful only as a paper-weight or doorstop without the software that lets it perform this or that task.

Finally, if you have your car fueled and ready to go, it is usually convenient to have a road on which to drive. Think of your Internet service provider (ISP) as the on-ramp for gaining access to the Internet.

Software—Your Browser

In order to go onto the Internet, you need an "Internet browser." An Internet browser is a program that allows you to see text, pictures, and video, and to hear audio clips (depending on your computer's capability), on demand, right at your computer. You can also use your browser, or a companion program, to send and receive e-mail to relatives and friends.

There are three leading candidates for your browser: Netscape Communicator, Microsoft Internet Explorer, and America Online (AOL).

"What is the difference between them?" you might ask.

Do you drive a Volvo or a Cadillac or a Ford or a Porsche? What is the difference between them? They all are designed to move you from *here* to *there*. One does it with more comfort, another with more road responsiveness. On one you may need to adjust the heat and air conditioning manually; another might have them thermostatically controlled. One might have cruise control; another requires you to keep your foot on the accelerator.

So it is with browsers. One handles a task *this* way. The other does it *that* way. But they both get you from here to there. Which one you use depends on which one you have access to and, when you become a more sophisticated user, which one you prefer. Either will serve you well. As of this writing, both Microsoft and Netscape give away their browser for free. If you purchased a new computer, you undoubtedly have one or both installed on it. If you do not have either browser, ask your Internet mentor which browser he or she recommends. Lacking a mentor, find out which browser your ISP recommends. ISP selection is covered in the next section.

America Online (AOL) purchased Netscape Communications late in 1998. As of this writing, AOL has its own built-in browser. It, too, serves to get you from here to there on the Internet, though it is unique to and customized for AOL. By the time you read this, AOL may have incorporated a version of Netscape into itself, rather than using its own, separate browser.

> Did you miss the news on the hour on the radio? Tune into abcnews.com and play last hour's news report whenever you want to hear it!

An Internet Service Provider (ISP)

Once you have your car (the computer) and you've filled it with gas (found and loaded your browser), it's time to get onto the Information Superhighway—the Internet!

To do so, you need to pay your way onto an "on-ramp"—an Internet Service Provider (ISP). An ISP is a company that sells Internet access. You pay them a fee so your computer can phone their computer, and they, in turn, allow you to go onto the Internet.

How Do I Find an ISP?

Here, too, you have a decision to make. A quick glance in the yellow pages under "Internet" for your town will undoubtedly show dozens, if not hundreds of ISP listings. There are also national ISPs seeking your business.

Generally, ISPs will charge a flat rate of between $15 and $40 per month for their service. For that amount you should be able to connect to the Internet for as many hours per month as you choose.

One excellent way of selecting your ISP is to ask around. Find out what service your computer mentor uses. What ISP do your friends use? Are they satisfied with it?

There are a number of criteria you can use to judge ISPs:

- Is it a local, national, or international business? Local ISPs can often offer more personalized service. Each customer is important to them, much like the small grocery store down the block.

- A disadvantage of a local ISP is that its service might be less consistent than large, national services. You *might* get busy signals when you dial your local ISP more frequently than if you call a large, well-funded service that has invested in many incoming phone lines.

- Does it have local (i.e., toll-free) phone numbers you can call to log on to the Internet? You certainly don't want to be charged for a toll call every time you access the Internet.

- How many incoming lines does the ISP maintain? The best service is of no use to you if your computer receives busy signals when you call in to get on the Internet. Find out the prospective ISP's list of dial-in numbers and over a period of a few days dial each number from time to time. Be sure to call during a time of day that is typically busy for an ISP, usually the early evening. If you frequently get a busy signal, so will your computer when it tries to phone in. You should hear the kinds of electronic beeps and chirps and boings you may have encountered when you have sent a fax in the past. They mean your computer will likely be able to set up an Internet connection when it calls.

- What sort of technical support does the ISP provide? Is there a phone number you can call for assistance? What is the average wait on hold before you can talk to a human being? How good are the technical folks in answering your questions clearly and helpfully?

> There is <u>no</u> topic associated with connecting to the Internet that cannot be explained to you in an understandable manner. If a technical support person on the other end of the phone line is unable or unwilling to help you with a problem, it reflects their inexperience or lack of skill, not yours. If you call your ISP's support line on a number of occasions and find you usually have difficulty understanding the answers given to you, it is time to find a new ISP.

- What hours/days is technical support available? The best tech support is of no use to you if your question arises at 9:00 P.M. and they closed at 7:00 P.M. If you tend to investigate the Internet on weekends, it is certainly convenient to have an ISP you can call on Sunday afternoon.

- Does the ISP have a website that provides helpful information to new users?

- How much does the connection cost per month? Is it competitive in the marketplace? Are there additional start-up fees?

How about AOL?

Chances are good that you have heard ads for America Online (AOL). AOL is an ISP and more. Joining AOL allows you to explore the Internet and also gives you access to AOL-based information on a wide variety of topics and in a variety of settings. You can read the latest news and discuss topics of national in-

terest in AOL chat rooms. Investigate AOL "channels" devoted to sports, finance, computing, entertainment, lifestyles, health, and much more. You should note, however, that these AOL channels are *internal* to AOL and *not* the same as investigating websites devoted to these topics on the Internet. AOL offers you a selection of information, much more of which is available on the Internet. However, for newcomers to Internet investigation, AOL may be a good option. It has a relatively easy-to-use set of screens, its e-mail program works just fine, and it does allow you to browse the Internet, albeit sometimes with a slower access speed than a dedicated ISP can provide.

What's This I Hear about Viruses?

Computer viruses are small programs that are created by computer programmers whose intents range from mischievous to malicious. Viruses can be transmitted to your computer over the Internet. Since you are going to begin investigating the Internet, you should *absolutely* invest in a good antivirus program.

There are a number of good antivirus programs available on the market. Talk with your computer tutor/mentor about which program he or she can recommend. Currently, the leading contenders in the antivirus field are the Norton Antivirus program from Symantec Corporation and McAfee VirusScan.

Refer to Chapter 9 for more information on antivirus programs.

Next Steps

Once you (and your computer mentor) get your system up and running, go on to the next chapter. You're ready to take your first strides onto the Internet. Prepare yourself to be amazed at what you can do!

Chapter 3

Make Your First Connection

You have the gadgetry necessary to connect to the Internet. You have it hooked up. Perhaps you've watched as your coach logged on a first time to make sure everything is working correctly.

It's time for you to take over the controls—the keyboard and mouse or your WebTV control—and to take your first solo electronic steps onto the Information Superhighway.

Before we get started, the table at the right describes a few terms you will encounter in this chapter.

Logging On

Depending on which browser you've chosen (or which is already installed on your computer), you should have an icon on your desktop for either Netscape Communicator, Internet Explorer, or AOL:

Double click on the icon to launch your web browser. Then connect to your ISP, if it's not done automatically. Your computer mentor should assist you in doing that, if necessary. If you are using WebTV, activate your system and go online, using the instructions included with your system.

Depending upon which of the programs you use to access the Internet, you will be viewing a different screen at this point. In the case of Netscape and Internet Explorer, you can refer to this screen as your browser's "home page."

Jargon

Log on
To connect your computer to the Internet.

Go online
The same thing—you're about to enter the Information age!

Web page
One page of information (text, graphics, and perhaps music, video, or other multimedia pieces).

Website
A collection of possibly many Web pages, put up on the Internet either by individuals or organizations.

Hyperlink
A hyperlink is an area of a web page (it can be text or a picture) which, when clicked, will take you either to another web page or to a particular area of the web page you're looking at.

On AOL, it is the main AOL welcome screen. This is the screen that pops up by default each time you log on to the Internet.

For the purpose of beginning to explore the Internet, it would be helpful if you were on a particular website.

At the top of the Netscape Communicator screen is an area that looks like this:

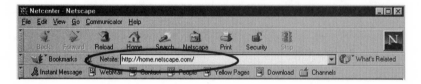

Notice the **Netsite** area of the screen, circled above. On your screen it may have something different than the `http://home.netscape.com`, shown above. If you are using Internet Explorer, the top of your screen should look like this:

Notice the **Address** area of the screen, circled above. On your screen it may contain something different than `http://microsoft.com/MS.htm`, as shown here.

If you are using AOL, the top of your screen will look like this:

Notice the circled area of the AOL screen above.

Whichever browser you are using, click your mouse in the area of the screen that is circled above. That should highlight the entire text currently in that area in reverse colors, like this:

`Type Keyword or Web Address here and click Go`

If your text is not highlighted in reverse colors as shown here, move the mouse to the end of the text now in the box (`http://home.netscape.com`, `http://microsoft.com/ms.htm` or "Type Keyword or Web Address here and click Go" in the examples shown above). Press and hold down the *left* mouse button. Use your mouse to drag the cursor on the screen to the left, keeping the left button pressed, until all of the words are highlighted, as shown above. Then release the button.

In Windows terminology, pressing and holding down the left mouse button and moving your cursor across text is called "selecting text" or "dragging across text."

Apple computer mice have only one button. Use that button in exactly the same manner as described here for the left button on PC mice.

Now, type:

`cnn.com`

Note: It doesn't matter if you type this in capital or lowercase letters. They are interchangeable.

Finally, press ENTER on your keyboard and you should be taken to the main page of the CNN website.

Tip

I want to repeat an important point to keep in mind as you begin your exploration of the Internet:

You cannot break anything—neither on your computer nor on any other one—by pushing any button on your computer or by clicking on anything on the screen. So don't worry. You cannot do anything wrong. You may not always accomplish what you set out to do, but you cannot do anything irrevocable. Relax and enjoy yourself!

URL—Didn't I Go to High School with Him?

The web address `cnn.com` is also called the "URL" for the Cable News Network, CNN. URL stands for "Uniform Resource Locator" or "Universal Resource Locator." Every web page has its own URL, its own unique electronic address.

There is no agreement yet among Internet users regarding the pronunciation of "URL." Many pronounce it "Earl," and many pronounce it by spelling it out, "U, R, L." It is even occasionally pronounced like the name of the Ural mountains in Russia. I tend to refer to it as just a "web address," as in, "Would you e-mail me the web address for that site?" Use whatever feels comfortable for you.

You should now see the CNN main web page on your screen. Up near the top of the screen where you typed in `cnn.com`, your web browser has expanded the URL for the website to either `http://www.cnn.com` or `http://cnn.com`; this is the site's full, official URL. Notice, though, that you got away with typing just the `cnn.com` piece of the URL. The rest is "Internet-ese," technical pieces that, while they are necessary, you need not worry about for now. The browser knows what you mean and automatically uses the full address. Once you have the CNN website on your screen, you should see today's news headlines appear. You won't be able to see all of the headline news on your screen. You can scroll downward to see more of it in any of three ways:

- Use the scroll bar on the right hand side of the screen to scroll downward (ask you computer mentor if you need assistance), or

- Press ⬇ to move down approximately one line of text at a time, or

- Press the [PG DN] to move down one screen at a time.

Hyperlinks

On the Internet, different web pages are often "linked" so you can get from one to the other more easily. You navigate your way from here to there by typing URLs and also through the use of what are called *hyperlinks*.

How Do I Move to Another Website?

Move your mouse around so the pointer on your monitor moves across the CNN web page. For now, don't click any button on your mouse. Notice, though, as you move your mouse, the pointer on your screen changes shape from time to time.

Sometimes it is shaped like this: ⬦

At other times it is shaped like the letter "I": ⌶

At still other times it is shaped like a hand: ☝

For example, use the mouse to move your cursor to the left of the CNN screen where you see the word "weather." When you move your cursor over the word "weather," you will notice it turns into the hand shape. Whenever your cursor is shaped like a hand, it is over a hyperlink. A hyperlink is an area of a web page (it can be text or a picture) that, when clicked, will take you either to another web page or to a particular area of the web page you're looking at.

> By the time you read this, the CNN website may have been redesigned. If "weather" isn't still on the left side of the CNN main screen, experiment with other hyperlinks. Move your mouse around until the pointer turns into a hand, then click the left mouse button.

You generally will know which words on a web page are hyperlinks because they will appear a different color from the other text on the screen, or they may be underlined.

Click your mouse on any hyperlink on the CNN web page. You will be taken to a new web page reflecting the hyperlink you clicked. This would be a good time for you to go ahead and experiment a bit; click on a hyperlink to get to a new web page. Look over what that page has to offer, then click on a hyperlink on that page to move to another. Visit a few different web pages in this way.

> You will definitely know when your cursor is pointing at a hyperlink, because it will take on the shape of a hand. Any time your cursor is shaped like a hand, it is on a hyperlink.

Take your time. Look over the information on a given page. Explore. Enjoy yourself—you've begun to browse the Internet!

How Do I Return to a Website I Visited Before?

Once you have done that for a few minutes, investigating page after page after page, you might want to get back to a previous page, or even all the way back to the main CNN page. Of course, one way to go back to the main CNN page would be for you to click up in the URL area of your browser and type `cnn.com` as before.

But what if you don't want to go all the way back to the main CNN page? What if you just want to go back to a web page you visited a minute or two ago?

The Back Button

Look at the pictures near the beginning of this chapter of the tops of the various browser screens. Notice on both Explorer and Netscape there is a button with an arrow pointing to the left that is labeled "Back." In AOL it is a button with a VCR-like arrow on it that is pointing left. All of these buttons allow you to retrace your steps from one previously visited website to the next. Click the **Back** button on your browser. You will return to the site you visited just prior to the one you're currently on. Click the button again and you will go back another step. If you keep clicking the **Back** button, you will ultimately return to the main CNN web page, having retraced your steps.

What if you get a little overly enthusiastic using the **Back** button and overshoot the website to which you wanted to return? Simple. Next to the **Back** button is a **Forward** button. In AOL, it is an arrow pointing to the right. That moves you forward, website by website, retracing your steps in the forward direction.

The History List

One more thing to try in Internet Explorer and Netscape: Instead of merely clicking on the **Back** button, click on it using the *right* mouse button. You will see a list containing all the web sites you have recently visited.

In Netscape, it looks like this: In Internet Explorer, it looks like this:

   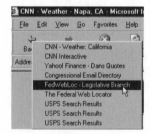

You can move back to any one of them by clicking (with the left button) on the site you want to revisit. The same technique holds true for the **Forward** button. These recently visited site lists let you leapfrog to a site, rather than retracing your steps one at a time.

You can accomplish the same task in AOL by clicking the drop-down arrow at the far right of the address area near the top of the screen and then clicking on whichever site you want to view again.

Bookmarks/Favorites

Move back to the main CNN web page, using one of the techniques listed above. Suppose you want to be able to return to this website easily in the future, without having to remember its URL, `cnn.com.` You can mark web pages for easy return in each of the three browsers.

Creating Bookmarks in Netscape

In Netscape, you create a "bookmark" for any sites you want to be able to re-visit easily. To create a bookmark for the CNN site, be sure you have that site displayed on your screen and then click the **Bookmarks** button near the top of your screen, circled here:

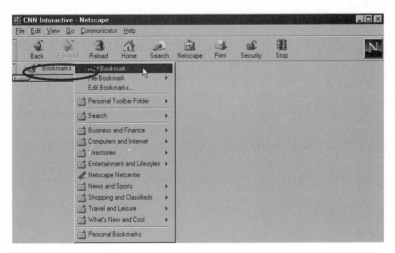

When you do, a menu like the one shown below will appear. Click **Add Bookmark** at the top of the menu. Once you do, the menu will disappear and your bookmark will be available to you in the future.

To use one of your saved bookmarks, click the **Bookmark** option. Your new bookmark will appear at the bottom of the menu, as highlighted above.

Any time you want to return to the CNN website, click that bookmark and you will be taken directly there.

Deleting Bookmarks in Netscape

From time to time you may want to delete a bookmark you have created. Perhaps you created it by mistake or perhaps the website is no longer of interest to you.

To delete a bookmark from Netscape, click **Bookmark**, the same button you used to create your bookmark. Select **Edit Bookmarks** from the menu that appears. You will see a screen similar to the one shown at the top of the next page. If you don't see your CNN bookmark on your screen, you may need to use the vertical scroll bar on the right side of the window to scroll down to the bottom of the list. Click on the bookmark to be deleted and tap DEL.

Tip

You can also add and edit bookmarks by clicking on the **Communicator** command on the menu at the top of the Netscape screen, selecting **Bookmarks** and clicking on either **Add or Edit Bookmarks** from the menu that appears. Alternatively, you can press CTRL + D on the keyboard to add a bookmark.

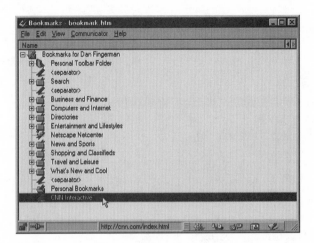

Creating Favorites in Internet Explorer

In Internet Explorer you create what is termed a "favorite" for any sites you want to be able to revisit easily. To create a favorite for the CNN site, be sure you have that site displayed on your screen, and then click the **Favorites** option on the Internet Explorer main menu, as shown here:

When you do, a menu like the one shown above will appear. Click **Add to Favorites** at the top of the menu.

Once you do, this **Add Favorite** dialog box will appear:

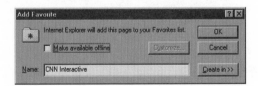

For now, just click the **OK** button in the top right corner of this dialog box.

To use one of your saved favorites, click the **Favorites** menu item at the top of the screen. You will see your new bookmark at the bottom of the drop-down menu:

Any time you want to return to the CNN website, just click that favorite and you will be taken directly there.

Another method for using your Internet Explorer favorites is to click the **Favorites** button on the toolbar at the top of the Internet Explorer screen. The button looks like this:

When you do, you will see a panel open on the left side of your screen.

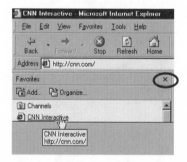

You can click on your newly created favorite, CNN Interactive, to be taken to that site. To close the **Favorites** panel on the side of your screen, click the **X**, circled above.

Deleting Favorites in Internet Explorer

From time to time you may want to delete a bookmark you have created. Perhaps you created it by mistake or perhaps the website is no longer of interest to you.

The easiest way to delete a bookmark from Internet Explorer is to click the **Favorites** option on the main menu and point at the favorite you want to eliminate. Click the *right* mouse button on that favorite. You will see a menu like this one appear:

Click the **Delete** option with the left mouse button and you will eliminate the unwanted favorite from your list.

Creating Favorite Places in AOL

In AOL you can create what is termed a "favorite place" for any sites you want to be able to revisit easily. To create a favorite place for the CNN site, be sure you have that site displayed on your screen. Next, click the heart-shaped **Favorite Place** button that appears on the right side of the CNN window:

When you do, this screen will appear:

Click the **Add to Favorites** button.

Another way you can add favorite locations to your personal list is to drag the favorite place icon, circled above (it looks like a heart on a page), and drop it onto the **Favorites** button on the AOL toolbar at the top of the screen. That button looks like this:

Your new favorite will appear at the bottom of your favorites list.

To use one of your saved favorites, click the **Favorites** button on the toolbar at the top of the AOL screen. When you do, a screen like this one will appear, displaying all of the favorite places you have saved, together with a few additional sites put there by AOL:

Any time you want to return to the CNN website, just click that favorite and you will be taken directly there.

Deleting Favorite Places in AOL

From time to time you may want to delete a favorite you have created. Perhaps you created it by mistake or perhaps the website is no longer of interest to you.

The easiest way to delete a favorite from AOL is to click the **Favorites** button on the AOL toolbar, shown above, and click on **Favorite Places**, the first item on the menu that appears. When you do, you will see a screen similar to this one appear:

Click the favorite listing you want to eliminate and then click the **Delete** button at the bottom of that window. That favorite place will be removed from your listing.

Next Steps

The skills you have learned in this chapter will open a world of Internet possibilities for you to explore. When you find sites that interest you, create a favorite or bookmark so you can access them easily in the future.

In Chapter 5 you will learn more sophisticated strategies for seeking out websites that are of interest to you, rather than just stumbling across them by accident. For now, though, allow yourself to wander, going where hyperlinks and serendipity lead you. You might even peek ahead into Chapter 10 where you will find a number of websites that might interest you. You will be surprised, and I hope pleased, by some of your discoveries.

Chapter 4

Send Your First E-mail

The Internet gives you the ability to send electronic mail (now commonly called "e-mail") to your friends. When you send e-mail, your message is delivered from your computer to your friend's—whether the friend is across the street or halfway around the world—virtually as soon as you press [ENTER].

You Know How to Send Mail

You've been mailing letters to friends for decades. First, you write the letter. Next you put the letter in an envelope and address it, provided, of course, that you remember your friend's address. If you don't, you get out your address book, look up the address, and then complete the envelope. Finally, you seal and stamp the envelope and take it to the mailbox on the corner. A day or two or five or ten later, your friend discovers your letter in the mailbox. Using the new jargon, this is called sending "snail mail." It will probably arrive, but it will take some time to do so.

Sending E-mail Is Not So Different

Sending e-mail is very similar to sending snail mail. You write your letter, using whichever web browser's e-mail tool is on your computer. Then you type in your friend's e-mail address. If you don't remember the e-mail address, either you look it up in your computerized address book, or you use one of the Internet-based search tools discussed later in this chapter. Finally, you click a button and off it goes. If your friend happens to be connected to the Internet (online) at the time, that person can open and read what you wrote within a few seconds of your sending it. If the person is not online, her Internet service provider (ISP) holds the e-mail until she next logs on to the Internet. Her com-

puter then announces, using one technique or another, that she has mail wait-ing. It makes no difference if your friend is across the street or across the world.

Similarly, when someone sends you an e-mail message, it sits quietly at your ISP awaiting the next time you log on to the Internet. At that time you will be notified that you have waiting mail, and you will be able to read it immediately or save it to read later.

How Do I Access E-mail?

This section will explain how to write an e-mail letter to a friend. As you saw in the last chapter, how you perform tasks depends on which web browser you are using. Refer to the appropriate selection below.

> Before you can send or receive e-mail, there are a few technical issues you need to deal with. These technical issues are quite unique, computer by com-puter and ISP by ISP, and are therefore beyond the scope of this book. I sug-gest you either enlist your mentor's help or phone your ISP technical support number to get their assistance in making sure that e-mail works properly on your computer.

Netscape Communicator/Messenger

Load Netscape Communicator, as you learned to do in Chapter 3. On the task bar at the bottom of the screen you might see a button that looks something like this:

If you do, click it to access the Netscape e-mail capability.

If that button does not appear on your screen, click the **Communicator** command on the main Netscape page, at the top of the screen:

Next, click on the **Messenger** command from the menu that appears to access the Netscape e-mail capability:

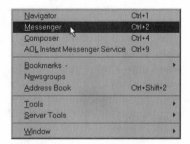

The Netscape **Inbox** window will appear:

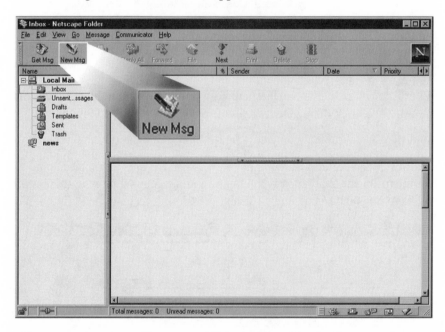

To create a new e-mail message, click the **New Msg** button near the top of the screen, and this **Composition** window will appear:

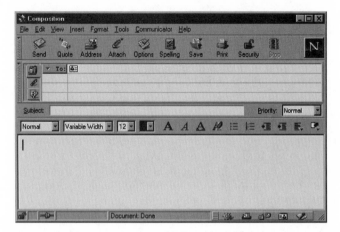

To learn how to compose and send the e-mail, skip ahead in this chapter to the section titled "Parts of an E-mail Address" (page 44).

America Online (AOL)

Load AOL and sign on, as you learned to do in Chapter 3. Once you have connected to AOL, click the **Write E-mail** button,

that appears on the toolbar near the top of your screen. When you do, you will be taken to the **Write Mail** screen, shown here:

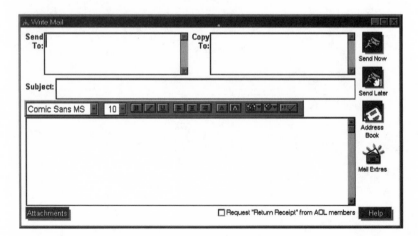

Now skip ahead in this chapter to the section titled "Parts of an E-mail Address" (page 44).

Microsoft Internet Explorer

Load Microsoft Internet Explorer, as you learned to do in Chapter 3. To prepare to send your e-mail, click the **Mail** button:

When you do, you will see a drop-down menu appear:

Click **New Message** and you will be taken to the Outlook Express **New Message** screen:

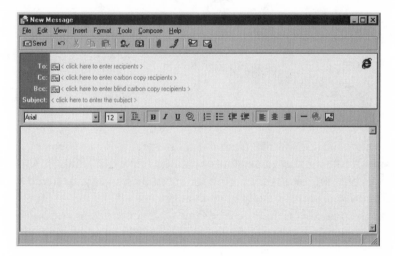

Parts of an E-mail Address

Think of a snail-mail address. Virtually any letter you address to an individual is made of the same component parts. For example, consider mailing a letter to your friend Arlene Bolin. You might address the envelope like this:

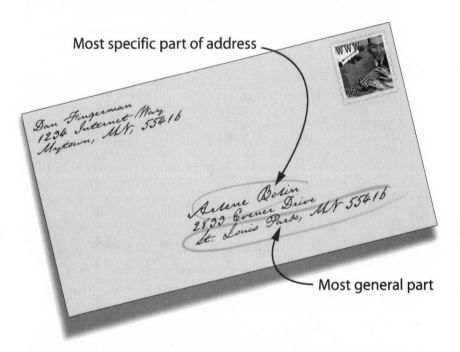

Most specific part of address

Dan Fingerman
1234 Internet Way
Mytown, MN, 55416

WWW

Arlene Bolin
2833 Evener Drive
St. Louis Park, MN 55416

Most general part

Snail-mail addresses move from the most specific (your friend's name or nickname) to the most general (state or country name). In addition, you probably would put your return address on the envelope, in case your friend has lost your address and wants to reply to your letter.

E-mail addresses work in much the same way. They, too, move from the specific to the general, only from left to right. Typical e-mail addresses might look like these:

- `bowler@blop.net`

- `president@whitehouse.gov`

- `hounddog@lonelystreet.com`

The first part of an e-mail address consists of the name ("bowler"), nickname, or other identifier (e.g., "president" or "hounddog") of the recipient. This part of the e-mail address is often referred to as the "username."

> Yes, that is one word—"username"—rather than "user name" with a space between the words. It seems that folks in the hi-tech industry have relatively idiosyncratic ways of spelling (e.g., Compaq), capitalizing and dividing words or gluing them together (e.g., SmartSuite or QuickBooks).

Unfortunately, e-mail addresses can't spread over multiple lines, as snail-mail addresses do. So, instead of starting the e-mail equivalent of the street address on another line, we use the "at" sign—@—to divide the username from the rest of the address.

Immediately after the @ sign, you type the electronic location of the computer that holds your friend's e-mail. In the examples above, those locations would be "blop," "whitehouse," and "lonelystreet."

Finally, you type a period (generally pronounced, for some reason, "dot," not "period"), and then the suffix that indicates the type of organization the location represents. Current location types include "org", primarily for nonprofit or general organizations; "com", for commercial ones; "gov", for governmental entities; and "edu", for educational institutions like colleges or schools.

Tip
Don't put any spaces in an e-mail address; they're not allowed.

Countries also have codes associated with them. For example, if you want to visit the official website of the British Monarchy, you would go to `http://www.royal.gov.uk`. The final "uk" means that it is located in the United Kingdom. An analogous site in Iceland would end in "is", and at the Vatican, it would end in "va". For a list of codes for all countries, see Appendix A.

(*) Capitalization doesn't matter in e-mail addresses. These addresses are all equally valid:

```
president@whitehouse.gov
President@WhiteHouse.Gov
PRESIDENT@WHITEHOUSE.GOV
PrEsIdEnT@WhItEhOuSe.GoV
```

By custom, however, addresses are usually written in all lower case letters, as in the first example above.

Subject Lines

Regardless of which tool you are using to create your e-mail—Netscape, Internet Explorer/Outlook Express, or AOL—there is an area at the top of the "create new mail" screen where you are asked to put in a subject line. E-mail protocol strongly encourages you to enter a subject line. But, as with Emily Post's suggestions, you are not *required* to follow the advice. Subject lines are not mandatory, but they are polite.

A subject line gives your e-mail recipient a sense, even before opening your message, of the contents of the e-mail she has received. For individuals who receive only a limited number of e-mail messages, subject lines may not be that crucial. However, for those who receive a lot of e-mail, a subject line like "Hi from Uncle Dan," or more specific, such as "lunch next week?" or "regarding order #445678," is helpful.

Type Your Message

In the main part of the e-mail screen is a large area in which you can type the body of your message. Use that section to express yourself as you would in a letter or a memo. Think of it as a blank sheet of stationery.

You may be familiar with word processing. Unlike a typewriter, you need not press ENTER at the end of each line of text. The same holds true for e-mail messages. You can just type away, and the computer will automatically wrap your words to the next line at the right time. You press ENTER only to designate paragraphs or to move down to a new line.

Spell Check Your Document

Each of the e-mail programs has a spelling checker (usually called a "spell checker") built into it. If you wish, it can scan your document for misspellings and help you correct them before the document is mailed to your recipient.

Be Sure Your Spell Checker Is Turned On

It is worth scanning your outgoing e-mail messages for spelling and typing errors before sending them. To do so:

- In Netscape, click on **Edit** on the menu at the top of the screen, then click **Preferences** on the menu that appears. In the **Mail & Newsgroups** category in the left window, click on **Messages.** If **Mail & Newsgroups** does not have the **Messages** option below it, there will be a small plus sign to the left of it:

Click the plus sign, then click **Messages.** In the dialog box that appears, you will see this line:

Be sure there is a check in the box at the left end of the line. If there isn't, click your mouse in that box to put one there. Finally, click the **OK** button at the bottom of the **Preferences** dialog box.

- In AOL, click the **Mail Center** button near the top of the screen:

Select **Mail Preferences** from the menu. In the dialog box that appears, you will see this line:

☑ Perform a spell check before sending mail

Be sure there is a check in the box at the left end of the line. If there isn't, click your mouse in that box to put one there. Finally, click the **OK** button at the bottom of the dialog box.

• In Outlook Express, click the **Tools** option on the main menu, then select **Options** on the drop-down menu. This dialog box will appear:

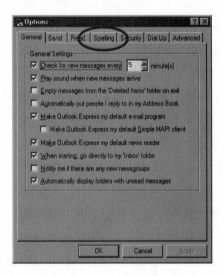

Click the **Spelling** tab at the top of the dialog box. On the screen that appears, be sure these two boxes are checked:

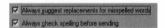

If either of them is *not* checked, click your mouse in it to mark it with a check. Finally, click the **OK** button at the bottom of the dialog box.

Outlook Express uses the spelling checker provided with all Microsoft Office 95 or Office 97 programs—Word, Excel, and PowerPoint. If you do not have one of these programs installed, the **Spelling** command is not available.

Try Spell Check

To experience a spell check in action, try sending a dummy e-mail message that includes a planned spelling error. Load your e-mail program, do not type an e-mail address or subject, but type the following line, including the misspellings, into the large area in which you type the body of your e-mail message:

```
This line is speled wromg
```

Now, to spell check in Netscape, skip to the following section. If you are using AOL, skip to the "AOL Spell Checker" section on page 50. If you are using Internet Explorer, skip to the "Internet Explorer/Outlook Express Spell Checker" section on page 51.

The Netscape Spell Checker

Click the **Spelling** button

that appears near the top of the **Composition** window. When you do, your spell checker begins to read each word in your document and check it against its built-in dictionary. When it reaches the word "speled," it realizes that it does not appear in the dictionary and presents you with options of what it *thinks* you meant:

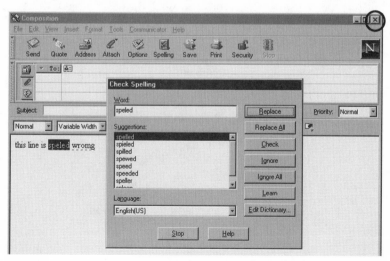

Since it has guessed correctly that you intended to spell "spelled," you can have it make the correction for you by clicking the **Replace** button on the right side of the **Check Spelling** dialog box. When you do, it will correct the misspelled word and move to the next one, "wromg." Again it will guess what you meant and assist you in spelling it correctly. The other buttons on the right side of the **Check Spelling** dialog box will be discussed later.

Finally, click the **Done** button. Since this is a dummy document that you want neither to send nor save, click the **Close** button in the upper-righthand corner of the window. It looks like a small letter **X**, and it is circled in the illustration above.

To prevent you from inadvertently deleting a message you want to save, you will be presented with this dialog box that asks, in effect, if you are serious about deleting your message.

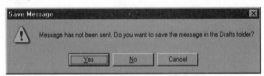

Click the **No** button to confirm that you want to throw it away.

The AOL Spell Checker

Be sure you have created a fake e-mail message containing the misspelled text "This line is speled wromg." Click your mouse at the beginning of the message, then launch the **AOL Spell Check** tool by clicking this button on the toolbar in the **Write Mail** window:

When you do, this dialog box will appear:

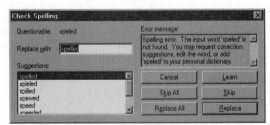

It indicates your misspelling and gives you a list of optional words that it "guesses" you meant to type. Notice that the correct spelling is at the top of the list—its best guess. Since that is the correction you should make, click the **Replace** button. You will be taken to the next misspelled word, "wromg." Again it will guess what you meant and assist you in spelling it correctly. The other buttons on the right side of the **Check Spelling** dialog box will be discussed later.

Finally, AOL will display a small box that tells you the spell check is complete. Click the **OK** button.

Since this is a dummy message, not intended to be sent, click the button with a small **X** in it at the top right corner of the **Write Mail** dialog box. Do not click the **X** button at the top right corner of the AOL screen, above the AOL triangle logo. If you do, you will close AOL and need to start it up again.

You will be asked if you want to save the message you are about to close. Click **No** to erase it completely.

The Internet Explorer/Outlook Express Spell Checker

Be sure you have created a fake e-mail message containing the misspelled text "This line is speled wromg." Click your mouse at the beginning of the message, then launch the **Outlook Express Spell Check** tool by clicking on **Tools** on the main menu at the top of the **New Message** dialog box and then clicking on **Spelling:**

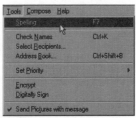

When you do, this dialog box will appear:

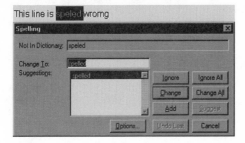

It indicates your misspelling and shows you what it "guesses" you meant to type. Since that is the correction you should make, click the **Change** button. You will be taken to the next misspelled word, "wromg." Again it will guess what you meant and assist you in spelling it correctly. The other buttons in the **Spelling** dialog box will be discussed later.

Finally, Outlook will display a small box that tells you the spell check is complete. Click the **OK** button.

Since this is a dummy message, not intended to be sent, click the button with a small **X** in it at the top right corner of the **New Message** dialog box.

You will be asked if you want to save the changes you have made to the message you are about to close. Click **No** to erase it completely.

Send Me an E-mail Message

It's time to send out what might be your first e-mail message. How about sending it to me? Seriously! I would love to hear from anyone who has made it this far into the book. Send it to my e-mail address:

dan@typewritergeneration.com

Remember, it's polite to put a subject line in your message. Let me know if this is the first (or second or twenty-fifth) e-mail message you've sent. I certainly hope that the volume of e-mail from readers makes it difficult or impossible for me to reply personally to every message sent to me, but I will promise to read every e-mail message you send to me at the address above. Feel free to send me your reactions to my book and any interesting stories about your use of the Internet. I invite you to share anecdotes, discoveries, frustrations, or essential information you have learned that wasn't covered in the book.

 Send me an e-mail message—really! I would love to hear from you. Mail it to me at

dan@typewritergeneration.com

Remember the Steps of Sending an E-mail

Regardless of the e-mail tool you're using, the steps for sending an e-mail message are the same:

1. Open your browser's e-mail program and indicate that you want to send a new message, as described earlier in this chapter.

2. Type in the recipient's e-mail address. In this case, type

   `dan@typewritergeneration.com`

3. Type a subject for your message.

4. Type the actual message content. In the e-mail message you are sending me, I certainly would like to see your name and the city and state (or country) where you live.

5. Finally, to send the message off to me:

 • In Netscape press the **Send** button

on the toolbar near the top of your screen.

 • In AOL press the **Send Now** button

   on the left side of the AOL **Send Mail** window.

 • In Internet Explorer/Outlook Express, press the **Send** button

   on the toolbar near the top of your screen.

6. If your spell checker appears, go through your document and correct any misspellings as described above. If it *doesn't* appear, congratulations. You spelled everything correctly, or, at least, every word you typed was in your spell checker's dictionary.

7. Your message should then be winging its electronic way to me!

For more information on working with your program's spell checker, please refer to Appendix B.

Replying to Messages or Forwarding Them to Others

There will be times when you receive an e-mail message and will want to type a reply back to its original author. At other times, you may want to forward an e-mail message, a good joke for example, on to some friends. Fortunately, performing both tasks is easy—no retyping necessary!

Netscape

In Netscape, to reply to an e-mail message you have received, click the **Reply** button near the top of your screen while the received e-mail is visible in the **Netscape Messenger** window.

Tip

If the sender of the message to which you are replying is someone to whom you are likely to write frequently, click on their name in the **From:** section of the message. Netscape will create a new address card for that person automatically, and they will be in your address book from then on. Refer to the section later in this chapter entitled "How Do You Keep Track of E-mail Addresses?" for more information on address books.

The original message will be displayed at the bottom of the **Composition** screen. You can type your response above it.

To forward a message to another recipient, just click the **Forward** button, circled above. The original message will not appear in the new mail screen, but it will be forwarded to the new recipient(s) whose e-mail address(es) you type in or add from your address book.

Outlook Express

To respond to a message using Outlook Express, click the **Reply to Author** button near the top of your screen while the message you received is visible:

The original message will be displayed at the bottom of the new document screen. You can type your response above it.

To forward a message to another recipient using Outlook Express, click the **Forward Message** button, circled above. The original message will appear at the bottom of your screen. You can type anything you wish to add above it. Also, you can go into the message you are forwarding and delete any excess information in it, like the list of previous recipients. Indeed, e-mail courtesy encourages you to get rid of such superfluous information before sending on messages to others.

Tip

If you use "Reply to Author" frequently for your own e-mail messages, you might want to remember the Outlook Express keyboard shortcut for it. Press and hold down CTRL and tap R .

America Online (AOL)

In AOL, to respond to an e-mail message, click the **Reply** button on the right side of the AOL message screen:

To forward a message to another recipient from AOL, click the **Forward** but-

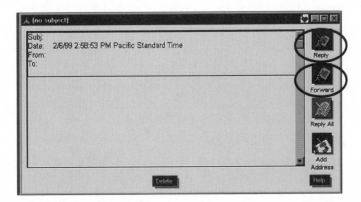

ton, circled above. The original message will not appear in the new mail screen, but it will be forwarded to the new recipient(s) whose e-mail address(es) you type in or add from your address book.

How Do I Locate Someone's E-mail Address?

Now that you know how to send e-mail messages, how do you find the addresses of people to whom you would like to write? As you might expect, there are a variety of methods for doing so.

Think about how you locate addresses for sending snail-mail letters. Then, we'll investigate the Internet equivalent.

- *Call the person on the telephone and ask for his mailing address.* You can certainly do the same for finding a person's e-mail address—call them and ask for it.

- *Look up your friend's name in your local telephone book and copy her address onto a slip of paper.* You can do the equivalent on the Internet for e-mail addresses. Furthermore, if your friend doesn't live in the same city as you, you don't need to go to the library to locate a telephone directory for your friend's city; telephone books for virtually the entire United States, and many cities in other countries, are available on the Internet.

- *Look up the person's name in the roster for some organization to which you both belong or belonged.* More and more, besides listing contact telephone numbers and addresses for members, rosters are including e-mail addresses to expedite contact.

  For example, if you are trying to locate an old college chum, try contacting the alumni association for your alma mater. It probably has a website. Many such organizations have developed a list of contact addresses, both physical and electronic, of former students.

- *Hire a private investigator to try to find that long-lost friend from decades ago.* Why not play detective yourself and try to locate someone using the resources available on the Internet? It may take a little effort on your part, but it can often be done.

- *Give up on ever reconnecting.* The Internet gives you so many ways of locating someone that you shouldn't give up on finding them.

Let's investigate some methods for locating individuals on the Internet.

Tools on the Internet to Find People

There are a number of websites on the Internet that you can use to track down e-mail (and sometimes snail-mail) addresses for people. You access them using your browser, as you learned to do in the last chapter.

Open your browser and log on to the Internet. In the URL field, where you type the Internet address you want to visit, type the following:

```
www.whowhere.com
```

It will take you to the WhoWhere? People Finder home page. It should look like the one shown here:

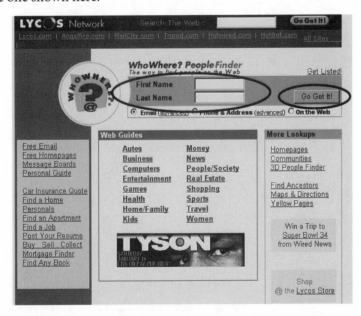

As an example of a search for a person, let's try to locate the e-mail address of Steve Johnson. Click your mouse in the **First Name** field of the WhoWhere? screen and type "Steve." Click in the **Last Name** field and type "Johnson." Be

Tip

WhoWhere! is not case sensitive when it comes to names. It doesn't matter if you type "Steve Johnson" or "steve johnson" or "STEVE JOHNSON." All of them will work.

sure the button to the left of **E-mail** is clicked (has a black dot in it), rather than the one next to **Phone & Address**. If **Phone & Address** is marked, just click in the circle next to **E-mail** to select it. Finally, click the **Go Get It!** button.

In a few seconds, WhoWhere! will give you the results of your e-mail search, which should look like the example shown here. The exact names you find might be slightly different:

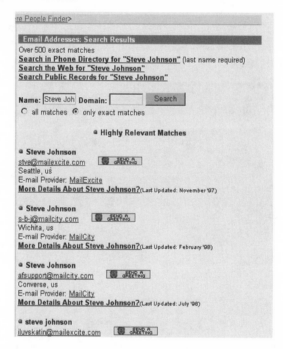

Notice that because you asked WhoWhere! to locate a relatively common name, it has come up with over five hundred entries. Perhaps the Steve Johnson we are seeking is the first one listed, at the Seattle address, or perhaps he isn't on this page at all. You can scroll down to the bottom of this web page, using either the vertical scroll bar on the right side of the screen or by pressing PG DN on your keyboard. At the bottom of the screen you will see this information:

> **Next 10 matches**
> **New E-mail Search**
> **New Advanced E-mail Search**
> **Add Your E-mail Address**

Tip

You can press the Tab key on your keyboard to move from field to field on a form like this one. SHIFT + TAB will move you in the opposite direction, field by field.

If you click on **Next 10 matches**, you will see the list of the next ten Steve Johnsons who were found. You could continue looking at the hundreds of listings until you found one who lives roughly where you think your friend lives, or perhaps you could proceed another way.

What more do you remember about your old friend, Steve? Is he "Steve" or "Steven"? Do you recall that he is "Steven M. Johnson," or "Steven W. Johnson"? The more you can remember about your friend, the more likely it is that you will successfully locate him in WhoWhere!

Suppose you look in your college yearbook and discover that he is "Steven W. Johnson." Modify his name where it (partially) appears in the field at the top of the WhoWhere! screen:

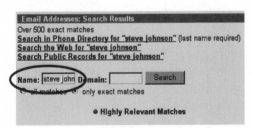

To do so, click your mouse just after the end of "Steve." You will see a flashing cursor appear. If necessary, move the cursor into position using the arrow keys on your keyboard, and modify the name. Part of the last name will slide out of view, but it will still be there. Finally, press the **Search** button again. When I conducted this search, changing from "Steve Johnson" to "Steven W. Johnson" narrowed my list from over five hundred to exactly four.

To complete the challenge of contacting your old friend, you can send an e-mail to any one or all of the located individuals by just clicking your mouse

once on their e-mail addresses. Doing so will open your e-mail program, complete with your friend's name in the address box. You can then type an e-mail message to one or all of the located individuals. In Chapter 1, I relate how my long-lost friend, Judy L., in Toronto, recently found and contacted me using exactly this technique. It works!

Other Good "People Finder" Sites

WhoWhere! is by no means the only way to locate friends. If you can't find someone using one of the search tools, try another. Don't give up! Other sites you might want to explore include:

- Four11 (http://www.four11.com/)

- InfoSpace (http://www.infospace.com/)

- Switchboard (http://netfind.switchboard.com/)

- AOL NetFind (http://www.aol.com/netfind/ emailfinder.adp)

- Yahoo! People Search (http://people.yahoo.com/)

- Netscape People Finder (http://home.netscape.com/ netcenter/whitepages.html)

How Do I Keep Track of E-mail Addresses?

How do you keep track of your friends' regular mailing addresses? Most likely, you record them in an address book. As you might expect, your e-mail program has an address book in which you can keep your friends' e-mail addresses. That way, once you locate someone's e-mail address, you can save it so it is readily available the next time you want to write that person.

Netscape Communicator/Messenger

To make a new address book in Netscape Communicator, click the **Communicator** item on the menu, then click **Address Book** on the drop-down menu that appears:

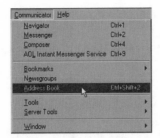

When you do, this dialog box will appear:

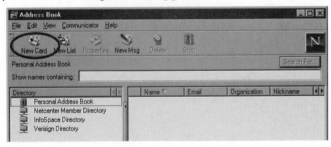

Click the **New Card** button shown above, and you will see a blank version of this screen:

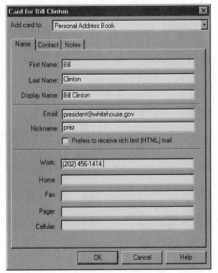

Fill in the information as shown above, clicking or pressing TAB to move from field to field.

The purpose of the nickname field is to allow you to access e-mail addresses more easily. In this case, when it is time to send an e-mail to President Clinton, instead of typing `president@whitehouse.gov` into the addressee field, all you need to do is type in the nickname you have assigned him, "prez." Netscape will take care of the rest for you.

To complete the entry, press the **OK** button at the bottom of the **New Card** dialog box. You will then see the president's name entered on the right side of your address book.

Now, suppose you want to send an e-mail message to President Clinton. Since his name appears in your address book, you can click on his name to select it, then click the **New Message** button.

You will then be taken to the standard e-mail form for writing your message. For purposes of this exercise, though, click the **X** box in the top right corner of the e-mail form to close it without actually sending it.

If a friend's e-mail address changes and you want to update your address book, display the address book and either double-click on the friend's entry, or single-click on it and click the **Properties** button.

If you receive an e-mail from a friend, you can add that person's name and e-mail address to your address book by clicking on his name as it appears on the incoming message. You will be taken to a new address card that has been filled out for that person. Make any necessary adjustments and click **OK**. That person will be added to your address book.

To delete someone's e-mail address from your address book, highlight his name in the address book and then click the **Delete** button on the tool bar.

America Online (AOL)

To add to your address book in AOL, click the **Mail Center** button

at the top of the main AOL screen. When you do, select **Address Book** from the drop-down menu that appears:

When you do, this dialog box will appear:

Click the **New Person** button and you will see a blank version of this screen:

Fill in the information as shown above, clicking or pressing TAB to move from field to field.

To complete the entry, press the **OK** button at the bottom of the **New Person** dialog box. You will then see the president's name entered in your address book.

Now, suppose you want to send an e-mail message to President Clinton. Since his name appears in your address book, you can click on his name to select it, then click the **Send To** button.

Send To

Tip

If your recipient's e-mail address concludes with @aol.com (e.g. JaneDoe@aol.com), you can just type the beginning of the e-mail address, in this case, "JaneDoe". AOL assumes that if you do not put @ in an e-mail address, you are intending to send it to another AOL member.

You will then be taken to the standard e-mail form for writing your message. For purposes of this exercise, though, click the **X** box in the top right corner of the e-mail form to close it without actually sending it.

If a friend's e-mail address changes and you want to update your address book, display the address book and click on your friends' name. Then click the **Edit** button.

Edit

If you receive an e-mail from a friend, you can add that person's name and e-mail address to your address book by clicking on the **Add Address** button

appearing on the right side of your e-mail message screen. You will be taken to a new address card that will have the person's e-mail address filled out automatically. Add your friend's first and last name and click **OK.**

To delete someone's e-mail address from your address book, highlight his name in the address book and then click the **Delete** button

at the bottom of the address book screen.

Microsoft Outlook Express

To add to your address book in Outlook Express, click the address book icon

at the top of the screen. When you do, this screen will appear:

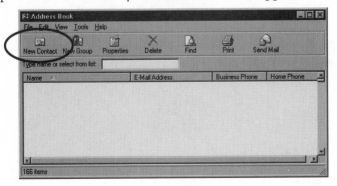

Click the **New Contact** button shown above, and you will see a blank version of this screen:

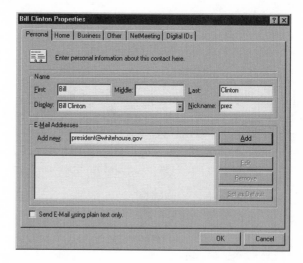

Fill in the information as shown, clicking or pressing [TAB] to move from field to field.

The purpose of the nickname field is to allow you to access e-mail addresses more easily. In this case, when it is time to send an e-mail to President Clinton, instead of typing `president@whitehouse.gov` into the address field, all you need to do is type in the nickname you have assigned him, "prez." Outlook Express will take care of the rest for you.

To complete the entry, press the **OK** button at the bottom of the Bill Clinton **Properties** dialog box. You will then see the President's name entered in your address book.

Now, suppose you want to send an e-mail message to President Clinton. If the address book is visible on your screen, you can click on his name to select it, then click the **Send Mail** button.

Send Mail

You will then be taken to the standard e-mail form for writing your message. For purposes of this exercise, though, click the **X** box in the top right corner of the e-mail form to close it without actually sending it.

If a friend's e-mail address changes and you want to update your address book, display the address book and either double-click on the friend's entry or single-click on it and click the **Properties** button.

If you receive an e-mail from a friend, you can add that person's name and e-mail address to your address book by right-clicking on his name as it appears on the incoming message. Select **Add to Address Book** from the drop-down list that appears:

You will be taken to a new **Properties** card that has been filled out for that person. Make any necessary adjustments and click **OK**. That person will be added to your address book.

To delete someone's e-mail address from your address book, highlight his name in the address book and then click the **Delete** button on the tool bar.

A Few Notes on E-mail Protocol

You should be aware of a few generally accepted "dos and don'ts" when it comes to sending e-mail.

- **DON'T** TYPE YOUR E-MAIL MESSAGES IN ALL CAPITAL LETTERS. Doing so is interpreted as the e-mail equivalent of shouting at the recipient. Of course, if you need to type in all capital letters because of visual limitations, by all means, do so.

Tip

If you know a person's name is in your address book, you can just begin typing either her first, last or nickname in the **To:** section of a new e-mail message. As soon as you have typed enough so Outlook Express recognizes who you intend to send your message to, it will complete her name for you. Then your ⌨TAB key or click your mouse to move to another field.

- **DO** spell check your documents before you send them. It's so easy to do . . . why not?

- **DO** use common sense. Do not write anything in an e-mail message you would not feel comfortable saying directly to the recipient. Unlike a snail-mail letter that you write, address, stamp, and then leave on the table by the door until you are planning to go to a mailbox, once you send your e-mail message, it's gone and irretrievable.

- **DO** be aware that, unlike when you speak to another person, whatever you e-mail to someone could be forwarded to a third party. Be careful what you put in your e-mails.

- **DON'T** give out personally identifying information like your home address, telephone number, or credit card or social security numbers to anyone whose identity you are unsure of. Alas, there are scams on the Internet, just as in the rest of the world.

Now, Go Connect With Friends

Now that you have the rudiments down, it's time to begin your e-mail experimentation. Be sure to send me an e-mail message (just one, please) at dan@typewritergeneration.com. Let me know how things are going as you begin to explore this newfangled realm of the Internet. If you locate and reconnect with old friends over the Internet, drop me a line and let me know. Who knows? Perhaps your "reconnection" story might find its way into a future version of this book!

Get out there and practice your new skills. Ask friends and relatives for their e-mail addresses, tell them what you are learning, and ask if they would be willing to receive an e-mail or two from you. If you have children or grandchildren in college or living far away, why not drop them an e-mail note to say hello? See if you can locate and reconnect with a long-lost somebody, using one of the "people search" tools discussed earlier in the chapter.

The world of Internet communication awaits you!

Chapter 5

Finding Websites That Interest You

By now you have begun to explore the Internet on your own. You've probably seen the vast array of information available to you out there. The question now arises, how do you begin to navigate your way through what are literally millions of websites on the Internet? How do you begin to locate those websites that are of real interest to you? How do you overcome or, better yet, avoid the frustration inherent in receiving too much superfluous information when conducting a search?

Think of walking into a huge public library. One way to locate books of particular interest to you would be to walk into the stacks and begin browsing. While that might lead to some interesting intellectual detours, it would be a relatively inefficient technique for finding information on a specific topic.

Similarly, while browsing the Internet might result in locating some interesting information, it is a highly inefficient method for locating websites of significance to you.

Back in the library, you probably would begin your search by heading toward the card catalog or, more common these days, the computer database. There you might look up some specific keywords that would allow you to focus on books or journals specifically related to your area of interest. Similarly, you can use any of a number of Internet websites, termed "search engines," to locate websites of interest.

Before we begin, the "Jargon" box explains some of the terms you will encounter in this chapter.

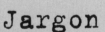

Jargon

Search
 Locate Internet websites that are of interest to you.

Search Engine
 An Internet tool that you can use to locate websites of interest to you.

Meta-search Engine
 A search engine's search engine. A meta-search engine is one that searches other search engines. The advantage of using a meta-search engine is that you have a wider net in which to trap your query. The disadvantage of using one is that you may end up finding more useless websites than you might otherwise.

An Overview of Searching

To conduct an efficient search for websites, you must first have clearly in mind what you're looking for. The better you can define your search, the more accurately any search engine will be able to locate websites of interest to you.

Suppose, for example, you are looking for information on the Oregon Shakespeare Festival, held annually in Ashland, Oregon. If you were to go to any search engine and type in the word "Shakespeare," you would probably receive information on thousands, if not hundreds of thousands of websites that contain that word. You would receive information on websites dealing with Shakespeare's life and times, websites dealing with his writings, websites dealing with college courses on his literature, as well as theatrical websites discussing or reviewing his plays. Keep in mind, these websites could and would be from all over the world. It makes no difference to the Internet whether the Shakespearean website is in Manhattan, Minneapolis, Melbourne, or Moscow.

To conduct a more accurate search, you could use a number of search terms in the search engine. For example, you could look not only for "Shakespeare" but also for "Oregon." By doing so, you are instructing the Internet search engine to locate only websites that contain *both* words. Some of the websites located would undoubtedly be for the Oregon Shakespeare Festival; however, others might well be for Shakespearean courses being taught in the state.

The best search of all would be one in which you asked the search engine to locate websites that contain the exact phrase "Oregon Shakespeare Festival." That should result in a list of websites that are mostly in and around the city of Ashland. You will find information on theaters, schedules, lodgings, and more. Of course, the list might include other related but less directly relevant information such as reviews of the plays performed at the Oregon Shakespeare Festival but that are reported in the *New York Times* or the *San Francisco Chronicle*.

How Do I Conduct a Search?

Think of an index at the end of a book. Broken down by keyword, it contains "pointers" to the page(s) on which a particular topic appears. Internet search engines perform much the same function. It is just that they point at websites that contain certain terms, rather than to pages in a book.

Most search engines behave in much the same manner. They send out automated indexing "robots" that are designed to travel to as many web pages as possible and index the words on those pages. The search engine adds the newly indexed entries to its existing database. So if, for example, a robot locates the word "Shakespeare" on a newly created web page at, say, `http://www.blop.edu`, the next time you perform a search for "Shakespeare" using that search engine, that website will appear in the results.

There are numerous search engines available to you, each having strengths and certain weaknesses. Let's explore two of the most commonly used search engines, Alta Vista and HotBot.

You will find, as you begin to conduct Internet searches, that locating information is no longer the problem; rather you will have to deal with receiving too much information—information overload. You will need to develop a skill that many of us never developed during our school days: formulating your questions and searches precisely enough that you don't get overloaded with information. You will learn skills and tips for conducting effective searches throughout this chapter.

> As you begin to learn to search the Internet, you will very likely be faced with the problem of receiving too much information. Don't despair! Practice, practice, and more practice will help you hone your Internet search skills.

Alta Vista—Conducting a Basic Search

When you visit `http://altavista.com`, you'll see a screen much like this one:

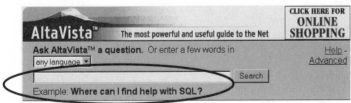

Type the word "Shakespeare" into the text box, circled above, and then click the **Search** button. In a few moments you will see the results of your search, much like the ones shown here:

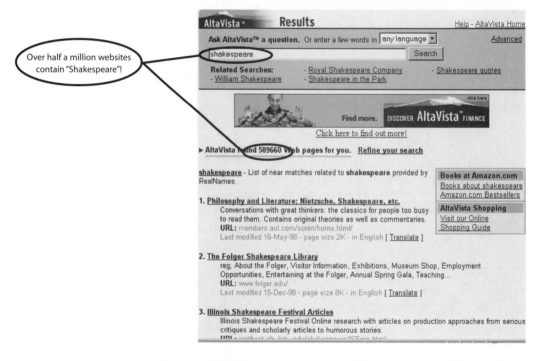

If you scroll down to the bottom of the screen, you will see information similar to the following:

As with any hyperlink you have visited thus far, to go to any of the located websites, put your mouse on the website you want to see and click once. You'll be taken directly to that website. To return to your Alta Vista search results at any time, click the **Back** button on your browser once or multiple times, as appropriate.

Study these two screens for a moment. Remember, you asked Alta Vista to locate "Shakespeare" in its index and report any website it finds that contains that name. In return, it reports that it has located over *half a million(!)* such websites. They are displayed for you in groups of ten at a time. You can see the next ten websites by clicking on page number 2 at the bottom of the screen.

Perhaps sifting through half a million websites to find out about the festival isn't what you had in mind. What if you try to refine your search by adding "Oregon" to the search box? The results yield good news and bad news.

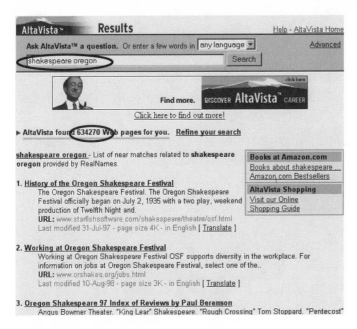

The bad news is that Alta Vista located 634,270 websites that contain "Shakespeare" or "Oregon," up from the 589,660 websites located on our previous search. The good news is that it located sites that contain both of those words in close proximity to one another, and it put them at the top of the list. Indeed, a scan of subsequent search page results indicates that virtually all of the entries relate somehow to the festival in Ashland.

Let's take the search one step farther. Suppose you're interested only in inns in the vicinity of Ashland. Add "inn" to your search list and see what happens.

Worse news! This search results in nearly *three and a half million* sites located.

Alta Vista—Refining Your Search

Recall that earlier in this chapter I mentioned "information overload." You have now witnessed this phenomenon firsthand.

Certainly the computer must be smart enough to sift through all this information for you and just give you the information that you're searching for—inns that are in and around Ashland.

Perhaps the **Refine your search** link, circled above, might yield some productive results in our quest for lodging in Ashland. Click it. When you do, you will see an Alta Vista screen, similar to this one, appear:

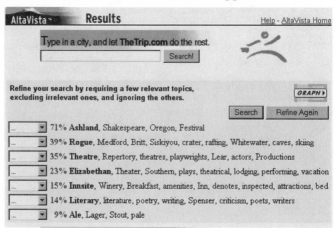

On this screen you can indicate which terms you absolutely want included and which you want excluded from your search. To do so, click on the small drop-down arrow adjacent to each of the terms, and select the appropriate option from the list that appears.

For example, we certainly want the Ashland option to be included, but since we are seeking lodging, we could probably exclude all websites dealing with white water rafting on the Rogue River. Continuing this thought process might result in the following selections:

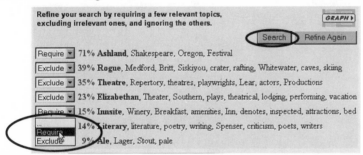

Finally, click the **Search** button shown at the top right corner of this dialog box, and you will receive a more limited selection of websites, in this case, all the way down to fifty thousand! However, after asking Alta Vista to conduct this search and upon reviewing the first fifty entries in the list, I find that all fifty of them are for inns in and around Ashland. Alta Vista has sorted the records in priority order, based on the criteria that we specified. Among those top fifty listings, you certainly should be able to locate one that meets your needs. Of course, if none of the top fifty do, you can still feel free to browse the remaining forty-nine thousand plus entries!

HotBot—Conducting a Basic Search

HotBot is another popular and powerful search engine that you can use to investigate searching and the techniques associated with it. When you get to the HotBot website, `http://www.hotbot.com`, you will see a screen similar to this one:

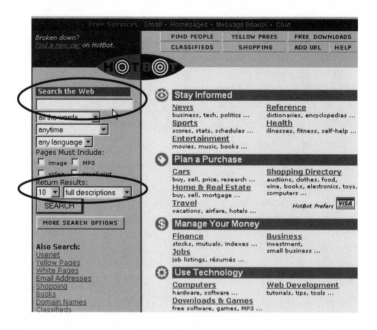

While the HotBot website offers hyperlinks to numerous features, listed on the right side of the screen, the deceptively simple-looking **Search the Web** section on the left hides a powerful set of search tools.

Let's continue the Oregon Shakespeare Festival example. Type that term into the HotBot **Search the Web** text box, circled above. After you press the **Search** button, you will see a list of ten Oregon Shakespeare Festival sites appear on your screen, shown on the next page.

Notice the circled section that reads "Get the Top 3 Most Visited Sites for 'Oregon Shakespeare . . .'" HotBot implements an interesting technology that is called **Direct Hit Popularity Engine**. This tool compares your search with similar searches others have made in the past then it provides a list of websites that these previous searchers have chosen to visit. These most-frequently visited websites can be accessed by clicking on the hyperlink.

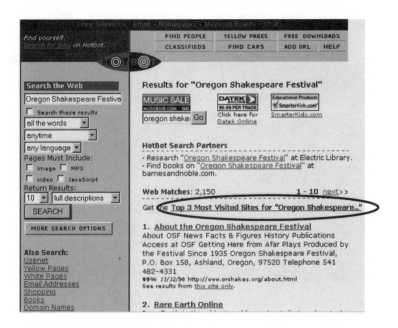

HotBot—Refining Your Search

Of course, you can refine your HotBot search in many ways. Again, remember that we're looking for inns in and around the Ashland area. Let's refine our search so HotBot gives us results that are more related to what we are seeking.

Perhaps the easiest way to start to this new search is simply to append the term "inn" to the end of this string of text for which HotBot is searching:

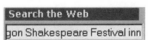

Once you click **Search**, you see a list of inns in and around Ashland.

HotBot also gives you a variety of other techniques you can use to refine your searches. For example, suppose you want a use the Internet to plan a tour of

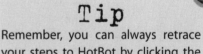

Tip

Remember, you can always retrace your steps to HotBot by clicking the **Back** button on your browser.

Alaska. Use HotBot to search for the words "tour" and "Alaska." You will see results similar to this:

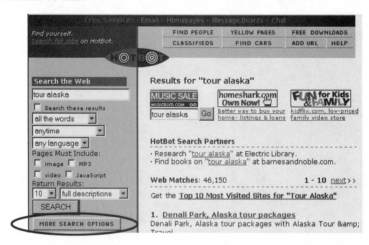

Once you scan the first few websites listed, you are reminded of the fact that your travel companion dislikes cruises. Perhaps there is a way to ask HotBot to locate Alaska tours, but eliminate all those that include a cruise segment. Fortunately, HotBot gives you an easy way to do so.

Click the **More Search Options** button, circled above. When you do, you will see a screen like the one shown here:

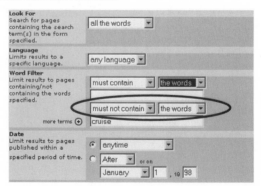

Note that there is an area in the **Word Filter** section that directs HotBot to ignore websites containing the word "cruise." Once you make that entry and scroll to the bottom of the screen, you can click the **Search** button. The results will be tours of Alaska that do not contain any reference to a cruise.

You can see that by combining HotBot's powerful search tools with a little creativity, you can quickly narrow your search to focus on the information you need and want.

As with any new skill, the more you practice, the more proficient you will become. Practice searching for topics that are of interest to you. The more you do it, the more accurately you will be able to search in the future.

Some Other Search Hints

As you become a more experienced Internet searcher, your skills will improve. In the meantime, HotBot has developed some strategies for you to consider when you need to perform searches:

- Use the most specific search terms possible. Instead of just saying "rice" and "menu," try putting in a list of four or five major ingredients that you would like to include in your recipe.

- Be as descriptive as possible. Be specific. Use synonyms. Use obscure terms if you can.

- A trick that some librarians use to come up with effective keywords is to imagine the ideal article on your topic, then formulate a headline for it.

- Search for exact phrases. In HotBot, you can type in a phrase and then select **exact phrase** from the drop-down menu that typically displays **all the words**. Alternatively, to have any search engine treat a number of words as a phrase, put those words inside quotation marks before conducting the search.

- Enter synonyms, alternate spellings, and various word forms (e.g. swim, swims, swimming.)

Other Search Engines You Should Try

All search engines do keyword searches against a database, but various factors affect the results for each search engine. Sizes of the databases, the frequency with which the databases are updated, and speed all contribute to remarkably different results. Also, different search engines report their results using different formats. You should experiment with various search engines until you discover the ones that work best for you and the types of searches you conduct.

Here are some to try:

- Alta Vista (`http://altavista.com`)

- HotBot (`http://www.hotbot.com`)

- Ask Jeeves (`http://www.askjeeves.com/`)

- Excite (`http://www.excite.com/`)

- Infoseek (`http://infoseek.go.com/`)

- Northern Light (`http://www.northernlight.com/`)

- Lycos (`http://www.lycos.com/`)

- Yahoo! (`http://www.yahoo.com/`)

Meta-search Engines

Meta-search engines conduct searches of several search engines. Some of the best-known meta-search engines are:

- Metacrawler (`http://www.go2net.com/search.html`)

- Dogpile (`http://www.dogpile.com/`)

- Inference Find (`http://www.infind.com`)

Next Steps

It is easy to be overwhelmed by the sheer volume of information that is available on the Internet. Although wandering from web page to web page and clicking hyperlinks to move from here to there might result in some serendipitous discoveries, more likely you will simply become bored with the technology before long.

However, if you use the Internet to investigate topics that are of real interest, you will find that it can become a magnificent window to the world. Go search for topics that fascinate to you. Go search for topics about which you want to learn more. It's all out there—more than you ever expected—just waiting for you to discover it!

Chapter 6

Chatting Online

It is 5:00 in the afternoon, and I am typing away on my computer. Up pops a screen in the middle of my monitor, containing the words "Hi, Dad." For a pleasant change, my son appears to be sitting in his dorm room at college, perhaps even attempting some homework. He is at his computer and notices that I also am on the Internet. He decides to check in and say hello. What a delightful reprieve from work for me! I write a note back to him, and we begin an online chat. True, we use our keyboards rather than a telephone to conduct the chat, but the advantage is that our interaction is free (except for your regular ISP charges)—no long distance charges.

Online chatting can occur any time, day or night. All that is necessary is that two or more of you be connected to the Internet at the same time and that you have the software necessary to conduct the chat. Fortunately, chatting software is readily available on the Internet, generally at no charge.

Probably the best chat program for newcomers is one provided by America Online. It is called AOL Instant Messenger, or AIM. AIM is available at no charge and can be downloaded from America Online. While you can use AIM from within AOL, you do not need to be a member of AOL to chat with it.

Using AIM If You Are an AOL Member

If you use AOL as your Internet service provider, and have a relatively new version of the AOL software, you already have AIM on your system. To activate it, click the **My AOL** button at the top of the screen. Click on **Buddy List** from the options that appear:

When you do, you will see this screen appear:

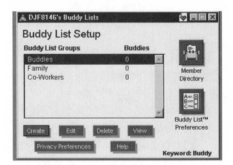

You will use this dialog box to create the list of your online "buddies" with whom you want to be able to chat. The list groups given are arbitrary categories. You can use the ones that are suggested—Buddies, Family, and Co-Workers— or you can delete some or all of them and create your own groups like Golf Partners, Art Collectors, or Punsters, as you will learn to do below.

Adding a Buddy to Your Buddy List

For now, suppose you receive an e-mail message from your niece saying how pleased she is that you are now online and inviting you to chat with her on AIM. She tells you that her AIM screen name is "joppa2833".

It is easy to add her to your buddy list. First, decide which group you want to add her to. In this case, add her to your **Family** group. Click on that group, then click the **Edit** button at the bottom of the dialog box. You will see this screen appear:

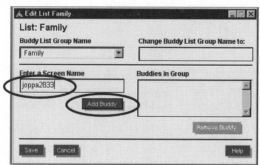

Type her screen name where indicated, and click the **Add Buddy** button. Her name will be added to the **Buddies in Group** list. Click the **Save** button and you will receive a confirmation that your niece has been added to your buddy list. Click **OK** to acknowledge the confirmation. Once you have done so, you will see that your family group now contains one buddy in the **Buddy List Setup** dialog box.

Creating a New Buddy Group

Suppose you would like to create a new buddy list group into which you want to place all of your chat friends in your neighborhood. That way you will know whenever any of them are online. For example, suppose you would like to add your friend, Alan, who lives down the block from you at number 923. When you saw him this morning, he told you that his AIM screen name is "alanat923".

To create the new buddy list group and add him to it, click the **Create** button at the bottom of the **Buddy List Setup** dialog box. This screen will appear:

Tip

If you know a friend's e-mail address, but not her AIM name, why not just drop her an e-mail note and ask for her AIM name? Of course, common courtesy requires that you ask permission before adding someone else's name to your AIM Buddy List.

85

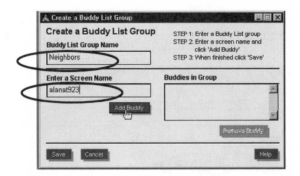

Type "Neighbors" in the field at the top of the dialog box and your friend's screen name, as shown here, and click the **Add Buddy** button. Click the **Save** button and again click **OK** to acknowledge the confirmation. You will now see the new Neighbors group appear at the bottom of the **Buddy List Setup** dialog box. It will indicate that you have one buddy in that group.

Once you have added all of the individuals you want to your buddy list (it is easy to add additional Buddies later in the process) click the small **X** button in the top right corner of the **Buddy List Setup** dialog box to close it.

Using Your Buddy List

Your buddy list window may now be visible on your screen. If it does not appear, click the **People** button at the top of the AOL screen and select **View Buddy List** from the drop-down list that appears:

In either case, a panel similar to this one will appear:

In this dialog box you will find a list of all your groups. In parentheses you will see two numbers, separated by a slash. The second number tells you how many buddies you have in that group; the first number lets you know how many of those buddies are currently online.

To learn how to chat with one of your buddies when they come online, look ahead in this chapter to the section entitled "Responding to a Chat Invitation."

Using AIM If You Are Not an AOL Member

You do not need to be a member of AOL to use AIM. Currently, AOL provides the service free of charge to anyone who wishes to use it. Many websites advertise AIM and make it easy for you to download it onto your computer.

If you cannot find AIM anywhere else, load your browser and go to the AOL website at `http://AOL.com`. At that website, you should see either an icon or a hyperlink that will allow you to download the latest version of AOL Instant Messenger. Click that icon or hyperlink and follow the directions that appear on the screen to download and install the program.

Once you have completed the installation process, either AIM will already be running on your computer, or you will see this icon on your Windows desktop:

If AIM is not running on your computer, click the icon to activate it. If you are not connected to the Internet when you click the icon, a connection will automatically be initiated for you. Again, follow the instructions on your screen for choosing a screen name for yourself. For the examples that follow, I have chosen to use the screen name "Fingerman1".

Once you activate AIM and select your screen name, you will see a window like this one appear:

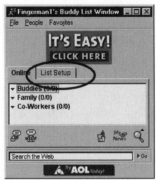

You will use this dialog box to create the list of your online buddies with whom you want to be able to chat. The groups that are listed originally are arbitrary categories. You can use the ones that are suggested—Buddies, Family, and Co-Workers—or you can delete them and create your own groups like Golf Partners, Art Collectors, or Punsters, as you will learn to do below.

Adding a Buddy to Your Buddy List

For now, suppose you receive an e-mail message from your niece saying how pleased she is that you are now online and inviting you to chat with her on AIM. She tells you that her AIM screen name is "joppa2833".

It is easy to add her to your buddy list. First, click the **List Setup** tab at the top of the AIM screen, circled above. This screen will appear:

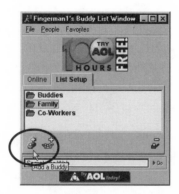

Then, decide which group you want to add her to. In this case, add her to your **Family** group. Click on that group, then click the **Add a Buddy** button, circled above. When you do, you will see a **New Buddy** indicator under the **Family** group:

Press DEL once and type in your niece's screen name, joppa2833, and press ENTER. She will be added to your list of AIM buddies. Once you have done so, click the **Online** tab on the AIM screen.

You will see the notation after your **Family** group "(0/1)":

That indicates that your **Family** group has one member listed in it, and that person is not currently online.

Adding a Buddy to Your Buddy List
If You Only Know His E-mail Address

There certainly may be times when you know a person's e-mail address, but you do not know whether that person is a member of AIM. Fortunately, it is easy to determine whether a person with a particular e-mail address also uses AIM for chatting.

Suppose, for example, you recently received an e-mail message from an old friend, whose e-mail address is uff@olinger.com. To find out if he is on AIM, click **People** on the menu at the top of the **Buddy List** window. Select **Find a Buddy** from the drop-down menu and then choose **By E-mail Address** from the submenu that appears.

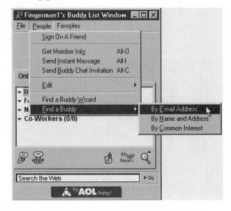

In the next window that appears,

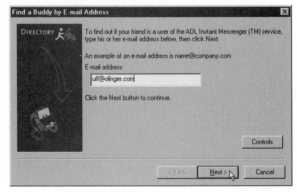

type your friend's e-mail address and then click the **Next** button at the bottom of that dialog box.

If your friend is registered as an AIM user, a screen similar to this one will appear with your friend's AIM screen name:

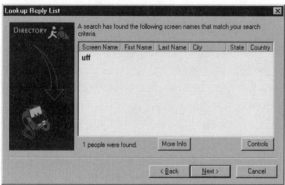

You can then enter your friend's screen name into your buddy list, as you learned to do earlier. If your friend is not currently an AIM user, another screen will appear that will allow you to send your friend an invitation to join AIM along with all of the necessary information for him to do so.

Creating a New Buddy Group

Suppose you want to create a new buddy group for all of your chat friends in your neighborhood. For example, suppose you would like to add to the list your friend, Alan, who lives down the block from you at number 923. When you saw him this morning, he told you that his AIM screen name is "alanat923".

To create the new buddy group and add him to it, click the **Add a Group** button that appears at the bottom of the **List Setup** screen:

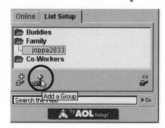

Type in the word "Neighbors" where **New Group** appears. Then click the **Add a Buddy** button to add your neighbor's name to the list, as discussed above.

Responding to a Chat Invitation

To chat online, you must not only have AIM installed on your computer, but also have it functioning while you are on the Internet. Look in the bottom right corner of your screen when you are logged on to the Internet. You should see the yellow AIM Messenger 🏃 near your computer's clock.

If you do not see him there, load AIM either by using the **Start** button and loading the program in the same way as you load others, or minimize windows until you can see your desktop and click the AIM icon that should appear there.

Once AIM is running, and you have informed friends and relatives that you are available to chat, you might find a screen like this one appearing on your monitor one day:

You recognize the user name "DJF8146" as belonging to your nephew, who is off at college. Type your response in the box at the bottom of the screen and press either ENTER or the **Send** button, in the bottom right corner, to send your response to him. Wait for his response, and off you go! Before long, you will have a dialog going like this:

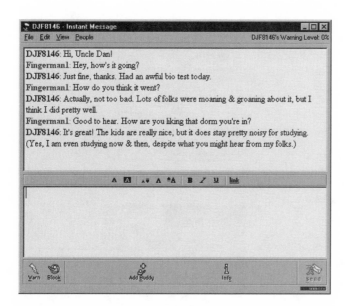

When you are finished chatting close down your AIM dialog screen by clicking the X button in the top right corner.

Chatting online allows you to catch up on all the latest news in your nephew's life in a casual, immediate manner. Do all of your young relatives pick up the telephone and call you as frequently as you might like? Unless you are very unusual, the answer is "probably not." They are, however, more likely to initiate spontaneous chats with you when they see you are online. This new technology fosters this type of spontaneous communication that otherwise might never have taken place.

Initiating a Chat

Whether you are in AOL or not, your buddy list will change when any of your buddies come online. If you are using AIM on AOL, your buddy list will look something like this when one of your buddies logs on to the Internet:

If you are using AIM with an Internet provider other than AOL, your buddy list will look like this:

In either case, to initiate a chat, double-click on your buddy's name and a message box will appear on your screen. Type in your message and click the **Send** button at the bottom of the message box. Your message will be sent to your buddy who can then respond to you, as discussed above.

(★) As you know, sometimes the telephone rings at inappropriate moments, and you are well within your rights to say you can't chat at that time. Similarly, common courtesy demands that you not impose on friends' online time without asking their permission first. An initial AIM message like, "Hi—it's Uncle Dan. Are you available for a few minutes to chat?" is completely appropriate. It's also important to respect your buddy's response when it is, "Sorry, I'd love to chat, but I just can't right now."

Other Chat Options

To be sure, AIM is not the only option that you have for chat software. A number of other programs are also commonly used to chat on the Internet. All of them are powerful and make your communications easy, but I feel that they are somewhat more complicated to install and learn to use than AIM. Still, here are some other choices for chat software for your future reference:

- ICQ (pronounced "I seek you") (`http://www.icq.com`)

- Microsoft Chat (`http://www.windowsupdate.com`)

- MIRC (`http://www.mirc.com`)

Next Steps

While chatting on the Internet is no replacement for a handshake, a smile, a wink, or a hug, when face-to-face communication is either impractical or impossible, it can fill the void. It makes no difference if your chat buddy lives on the next block or twelve time zones away from you. As long as you are both on the Internet at the same time and both use AIM or another chat program, you can stay connected and current with one another. Yes, the Internet can be used to bring people together, not isolate them from one another.

Chapter 7

Join Newsgroups

Has this ever happened to you? Some question or problem presents itself and you think "I bet someone, somewhere knows the answer/solution to that." But how are you going to find that person? If your question or problem is sufficiently unique or esoteric, it is probably unlikely that you will just "run into" that person without a fair amount of effort on your part.

Imagine that the bulletin board in your neighborhood supermarket restricted listings to only one topic area—a topic area of interest to you. Perhaps from time to time you attach a note to that bulletin board containing a question. Now suppose every other person in the world who is also interested in that topic shops at the same store and regularly reviews postings on the bulletin board, occasionally answering or commenting on questions that are posted there. It would, indeed, become a valuable resource.

Newsgroups (sometimes called "Usenet Groups" or "Usenet Newsgroups") are the Internet equivalent of such bulletin boards. There are literally thousands of newsgroups on the Internet, each devoted to a specific, often esoteric topic.

The Structure of Newsgroups

Newsgroups are arranged and named in a hierarchical order. The name of a typical newsgroup might be something like "rec.arts.theatre.musicals." In the newsgroup hierarchy, the highest order of information is the first section of the name, "rec," for recreational sites. Next come, in descending order, "arts," "theatre," and "musicals." Other "rec" newsgroups include such names as:

- rec.arts.books

- rec.arts.books.hist-fiction

- rec.arts.dance

- rec.arts.marching.drumcorps

- rec.arts.puppetry

Once you set up your computer to access newsgroups, as described in the following sections, you might want to browse through the list of available newsgroups. You will be amazed at the diversity of topics covered in the list.

Within a newsgroup are what are termed "threads." Harken back to the supermarket bulletin board analogy. Suppose you post a message asking whether anyone knew how to _____. Beth writes a response to your message, suggesting XYZ. Kevin writes another response suggesting ABC. You reply to Beth's comment and tell her that you already have tried XYZ and it didn't work. She then responds to your response, and so on. In the meantime, perhaps someone comments on Kevin's suggestion. You might view all of the interchanges like this:

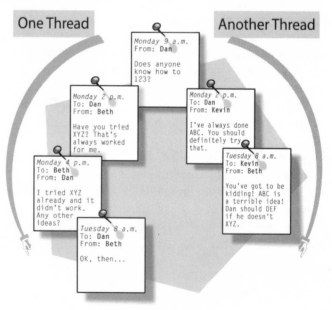

These exchanges constitute the threads of a discussion, and they illustrate exactly how newsgroup "threads" work, as well.

How Do I Get to Newsgroups?

Netscape, Outlook Express (Internet Explorer), and AOL all have the ability to display newsgroups for you. Naturally, as you've come to expect by now, each of the programs handles newsgroups in a slightly different manner. The next few sections will describe how you set up your software to access newsgroups. Refer to the following sections that are relevant to the software you are using.

Setting Up Netscape for Newsgroups

By now you should be fairly familiar with using the menus in Netscape. To set up Netscape Navigator so it can access newsgroups for you, click **Edit** on the main menu and then select **Preferences**. Click the small plus sign next to **Mail & Newsgroups**, as shown here:

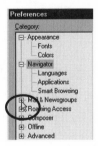

When you do, the list shown below will appear. Click **Newsgroup Server**. The right side of the dialog box will change, as shown. Click the **Add** button.

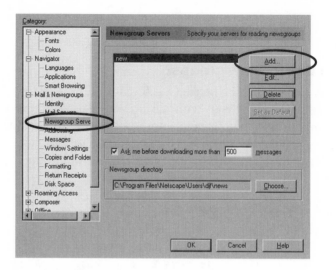

You may need to make a call to your ISP to ask for the correct information to put in the **Newsgroup Server Properties** screen that appears:

If, for example, your ISP is named `blop.net`, your server might be named `news.blop.net`. You can try typing that into the **Server** portion of this dialog box, and it *might* work. However, a call to your ISP will give you the definitive answer.

Once you have determined your news server information, click **OK**. You will return to the previous screen. Click the **Set as Default** button if the word **Default** does not appear after your new news server information. Finally, click **OK**.

To access newsgroups, click **Communicator** on the main Netscape menu.

Select **Newsgroups** from the drop-down menu that appears. You should see
your news server at the bottom of the list in the left-hand part of the window:

Before you can access newsgroups, you have to download them from your
news server. To do so, click on your news server in the left window, then click
on **File** on the main menu, then **Subscribe**. After some time, a list of the newsgroups will appear.

Now, move ahead in this chapter to the section entitled "Finding
Newsgroups of Interest" (page 104).

Setting Up Outlook Express for Newsgroups

By now you should be fairly familiar with using menus in Outlook Express. To
set up Outlook Express so it can access newsgroups, click **Tools** on the main
menu. Click **Accounts** on the drop-down list that appears. You will see this dialog box:

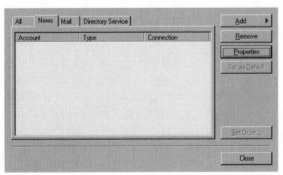

Click the **Add** button and select **News.** You will then be taken to the **Internet Connection Wizard.** Enter your name and your e-mail address in the first two screens you see, clicking the **Next** button in the dialog box each time.

You may need to make a call to your ISP to ask for the correct information to put in the **News (NNTP) Server** field in the **Internet News Server Name** dialog box that appears:

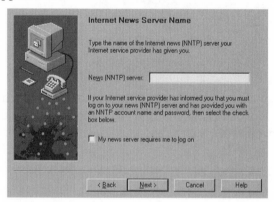

If, for example, your ISP is named `blop.net`, your server might be named `news.blop.net`. You can try typing that into the **Server** portion of this dialog box, and it might work. However, a call to your ISP will give you the definitive answer.

Once you have determined your news server information, click the **Next** button. On the next screen, type in the name for your newsgroup that you want to appear on your monitor. You can leave the default name for now by pressing **Next** again.

The next screen asks you to select the type of connection you will use to access your newsgroups. Generally, the first option, **Connect using my phone line** will be the correct selection for you. Again, press the **Next** button. Continue to move from screen to screen, and finally, click the **Finish** button.

You will see your new Internet accounts set up. Click the **Close** button in the bottom right corner of the **Internet Accounts** dialog box.

A dialog box will then appear asking if you would like to download newsgroups from your new news server. Click **Yes.**

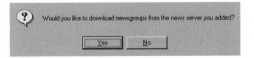

Now, move ahead in this chapter to the section entitled "Finding Newsgroups of Interest" (page 104).

Setting Up AOL for Newsgroups

By now you should be fairly familiar with using the menus and buttons in AOL. To use AOL to access newsgroups, click the **Internet** button at the top of the screen and click **Newsgroups** on the menu that appears:

If this is the first time you are using this AOL feature, you may see a message box appear that deals with filtering options. This feature allows you to filter out messages that you might find either irrelevant or offensive. For now, bypass this option by clicking **OK**.

You will be taken to a screen that looks similar to this one:

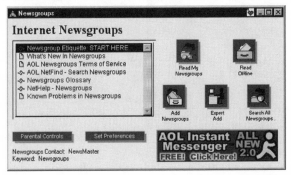

Now, move to the next section, "Finding Newsgroups of Interest."

Finding Newsgroups of Interest

As you know by now, there are a number of methods for accomplishing just about any task on the Internet. One excellent way to "get your feet wet" in your exploration of newsgroups is to load your browser and go to *Liszt's Usenet Newsgroups Directory* at

`http://liszt.bluemarble.net/news`

At this writing, that site claims to search 30,000 different newsgroups for topics that are of interest to you.

When you get to that website, you will see a screen much like the one that appears here:

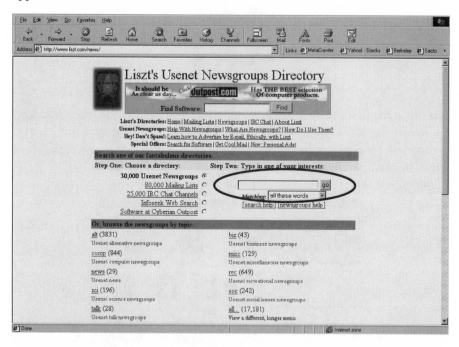

To use it, first be sure that **Usenet Newsgroups** is selected under **Step One**. Next, type the topic of interest to you under **Step Two**, circled above. For example, if you are interested in finding newsgroups related to bowling, type "bowling" in the text box and click the **Go** button. When you do so, a list, like this one, will appear.

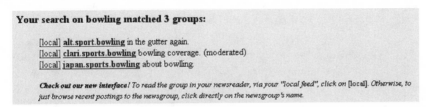

Your search on bowling matched 3 groups:

[local] **alt.sport.bowling** in the gutter again.
[local] **clari.sports.bowling** bowling coverage. (moderated)
[local] **japan.sports.bowling** about bowling.

Check out our new interface! To read the group in your newsreader, via your "local feed", click on [local]. Otherwise, to just browse recent postings to the newsgroup, click directly on the newsgroup's name.

Notice the message below the list of newsgroups. You have the option of either browsing through recent postings to the newsgroups or reading them in their entirety using your own newsgroup reader, such as Outlook Express, Netscape, or AOL.

You can also browse through newsgroups of interest. At the center of the main Liszt screen, shown on the previous page, you see a list of newsgroups broken down by topic area. If, for example, you click on **Usenet science newsgroups**, you will see a list appear like the one shown here:

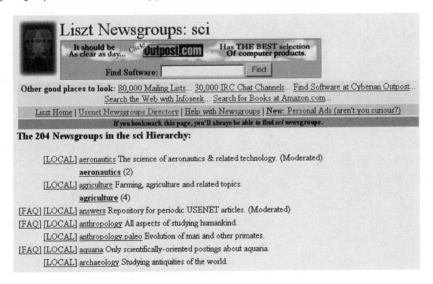

Liszt Newsgroups: sci

It should be   Click! **Outpost.com**   Has THE BEST selection
As clear as day...   Of computer products.

Find Software: [   ] Find

Other good places to look: 80,000 Mailing Lists... 30,000 IRC Chat Channels... Find Software at Cyberian Outpost...
Search the Web with Infoseek... Search for Books at Amazon.com...

Liszt Home | Usenet Newsgroups Directory | Help with Newsgroups | New: Personal Ads (aren't you curious?)

If you bookmark this page, you'll always be able to find *sci* newsgroups.

The 204 Newsgroups in the sci Hierarchy:

[LOCAL] aeronautics The science of aeronautics & related technology. (Moderated)
aeronautics (2)
[LOCAL] agriculture Farming, agriculture and related topics.
agriculture (4)
[FAQ] [LOCAL] answers Repository for periodic USENET articles. (Moderated)
[FAQ] [LOCAL] anthropology All aspects of studying humankind.
[LOCAL] anthropology.paleo Evolution of man and other primates.
[FAQ] [LOCAL] aquaria Only scientifically-oriented postings about aquaria.
[LOCAL] archaeology Studying antiquities of the world.

Notice that here, too, you can either display just recent entries by clicking on the newsgroup name, or you can choose to subscribe to the newsgroup using your software. You should also notice that a number of the newsgroups have **Frequently Asked Questions (FAQs)** associated with them, that you can read by clicking on the **FAQ** for each newsgroup.

Not all ISPs provide access to all newsgroups. If you learn about a newsgroup that your ISP does not appear to offer, you should send your ISP an e-mail message requesting access to that group. Generally, an ISP will be happy to provide you access if you notify them.

Subscribing and Posting Messages to Newsgroups

To see the content of newsgroups easily, you must subscribe to them. Doing so is easy in all three of the browsers.

Suppose you decide you would like to subscribe to the alt.sport.bowling newsgroup. The method is slightly different, depending upon which browser you are using for your Internet access.

Note that in this example we're looking for a newsgroup in the alt.sport (singular) collection. There is also an alt.sports (plural) collection of newsgroups. Be sure that you select the correct (singular) version in the examples that follow.

Subscribing to Newsgroups Using Netscape

If you are using Netscape as your browser, click the **Communicator** command on the menu at the top of the screen, then choose **Newsgroups** from the drop-down list that appears. A screen like this one should appear:

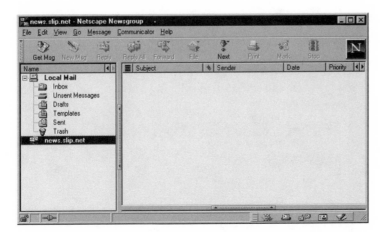

Click on the **File** command and select **Subscribe** from the drop-down list that appears. You will see a screen that looks much like this one:

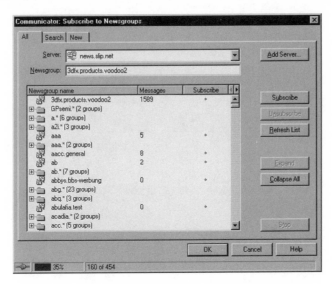

Scroll down the list until you see an indicator for alt.newsgroups appear:

Click the small plus sign to the left of the file folder. When you do, the alt group of newsgroups will expand, displaying the first of the second-level entries, as shown here:

Newsgroup name	Messages	Subscribe
⊟ 📁 alt.* (8991 groups)		
alt.-1d	6	•
alt.0.0.0.0.0.1.1.1.1.1.1.1.1....	2	•
alt.0000a.this-site.newgroup...	9	•
alt.0d	19	•
alt.1.aardvark	7	•
alt.12hr	6	•
alt.1d	16	•

Scroll down the list until you see alt.sport appear, then click the plus sign to the left of it, to expand that list. Scroll downward until you see alt.sport.bowling, and click on that. Then click the **Subscribe** button in the dialog box and finally click **OK**.

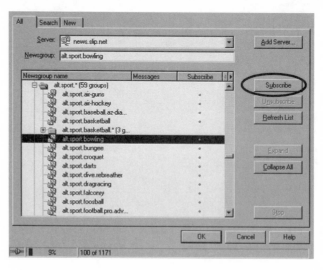

You will then be returned to the main **Netscape Newsgroup** dialog box, in which you will see the new bowling newsgroup appear in the left panel on the screen. After a few seconds, on the right you will see a list of messages that have been posted to the newsgroup:

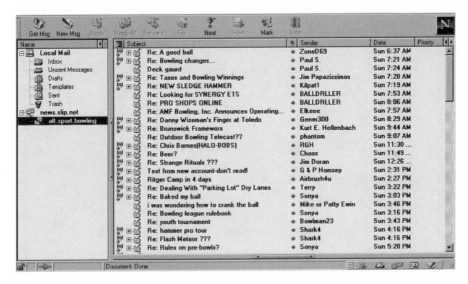

If you click on any of the plus signs next to many of the messages, you will see a list of threads arising from the main message.

Click on any one of the messages to read it.

Posting a Message to a Newsgroup Using Netscape

Suppose you now want to post a message on the bowling newsgroup. To do so, click the **New Msg** button near the left end of the toolbar. This dialog box will appear:

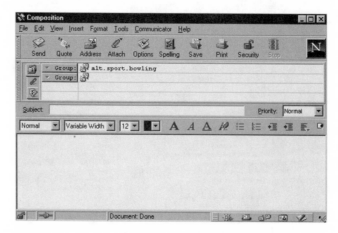

Type in your subject and your message and click the **Send** button. That's all there is to it!

Unsubscribing from a Newsgroup Using Netscape

To cancel your subscription to the newsgroup (also called "unsubscribing"), click on the name of the newsgroup where it appears on the left panel of the main newsgroup dialog box, shown above. Once the newsgroup name is high-lighted, press DEL to cancel your subscription.

Subscribing to Newsgroups Using Internet Explorer/Outlook Express

If you are using Outlook Express, at the bottom of the left-hand panel you will see an entry for newsgroups, as shown here:

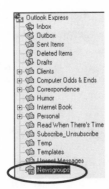

When you click on the **Newsgroups** button for the first time, this dialog box will appear:

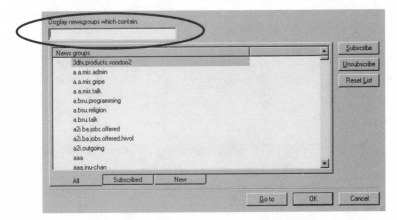

Click **Yes**. In a few seconds, you will see this screen:

You can also display the **Newsgroups** screen by clicking the **Newsgroups** button that appears on the toolbar at the top of the screen, whenever you have clicked on **Newsgroups** in the left-hand panel.

Since you know the newsgroup to which you want to subscribe, you can type its name, alt.sport.bowling, in the field at the top of this dialog box, circled above. Incidentally, it is interesting to stop typing for a few moments after you type just "alt.sport" and scroll through the list of newsgroups displayed. You will likely be amazed to see the diversity of newsgroups that exist just under this one heading.

After you have browsed through the newsgroups, finish typing "alt.sport.bowling," or click on it in the list that is displayed. Finally, click the **Subscribe** button on the right side of the dialog box. You will see a small icon appear next to the newsgroup to which you have subscribed.

Click **OK**. You will see the new newsgroup appear in the left panel at the bottom of the list. Click on the newsgroup in the left window, and after a few seconds, you will see a list like this one appear:

	Subject	From	Sent	Size
	Re: $ PROVA ANCHE TU $	KEGLEGUY	3/2/99 8:48 AM	9KB
	Re: $ PROVA ANCHE TU $	Jim Doran	3/2/99 8:22 PM	1KB
	Re: $ PROVA ANCHE TU $	KEGLEGUY	3/3/99 7:37 AM	1KB
	Re: $ PROVA ANCHE TU $	Pat Douglas	3/3/99 9:18 AM	1KB
	Re: 5-7-10 split @ Wis State Tourney (for NimBill)	NimBill	3/1/99 12:10 AM	1KB
	Re: 5-7-10 split @ Wis State Tourney (for N...	NimBill	3/1/99 12:14 AM	1KB
	Re: Adjusting onto oil for 2,4,7,8 pin	crazyjerry@my-dejane...	3/1/99 9:27 AM	2KB
	Re: Advise	BRNoCntrl	3/2/99 6:02 AM	1KB
	Re: Advise	Jay Walsh	3/2/99 11:12 AM	2KB
	Re: Advise	jayzin	3/2/99 6:42 PM	2KB
	Re: Another "myth"	Al Bundy	2/28/99 10:15 PM	3KB
	Re: Another "myth"	Ken	3/1/99 6:40 AM	2KB
	ASB---I Still love this thing!	John O	3/2/99 2:23 PM	1KB
	Re: Baked my ball	Dooby82Pen	2/28/99 10:18 PM	1KB
	Re: Baked my ball	NimBill	2/28/99 10:30 PM	2KB

From: crazyjerry@my-dejanews.com   To: alt.sport.bowling
Subject: Re: Adjusting onto oil for 2,4,7,8 pin

Outlook Express — Inbox, Outbox, Sent Items, Deleted Items, Drafts, Clients, Computer Odds & Ends, Correspondence, Humor, Internet Book, Personal, Read When There's Time, Subscribe_Unsubscribe, Temp, Templates, Unsent Messages, Newsgroups — alt.sport.bowling (298)

Compose Message · Reply to Group · Reply to Author · Forward Message · News groups · Connect · Hang Up · Stop

If you highlight a message in the top right window, that message will appear in the bottom right window on your screen.

Posting a Message to a Newsgroup
Using Internet Explorer/Outlook Express

Suppose you now want to post a message on the bowling newsgroup. Click the **Compose Message** button at the left end of the toolbar. This dialog box will appear:

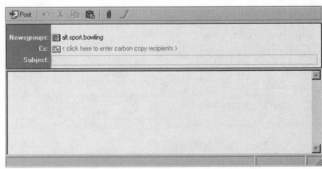

Type in your subject and your message and click the **Post** button. That's all there is to it!

Unsubscribing from a Newsgroup
Using Internet Explorer/Outlook Express

To cancel your subscription to the newsgroup (also called "unsubscribing"), click on the right mouse button on the name of the newsgroup where it appears on the left panel of the main newsgroup dialog box. Then click on **Unsubscribe from this** Newsgroup from the small menu that appears.

Subscribing to a Newsgroup Using AOL

If you are using America Online, click the **Internet** button on the main toolbar and select **Newsgroups** from the menu that appears:

A screen like this one will appear:

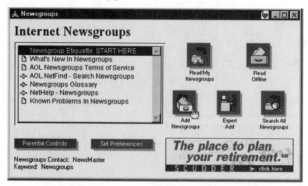

Click the **Add Newsgroups** button. You will see a screen like this one:

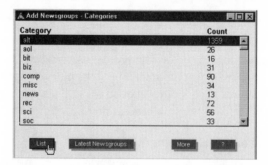

Remember, you're trying to subscribe to alt.sport.bowling. Notice that alt is already selected at the top of this dialog box. Click the **List** button at the bottom of the dialog box. After a few seconds, a list of alt topics will appear. Scroll down the list until you find alt.sport. Click on it and then click the **List** button again.

> Notice that the alt newsgroups are listed alphabetically. You may need to click the **More** button at the bottom of the dialog box if alt.sport does not appear in the original list of newsgroups.

Continue "drilling down" through the newsgroup hierarchy until you locate and highlight alt.sport.bowling. Then click the **Subscribe** button at the bottom of the dialog box. AOL will confirm your subscription by displaying a small dialog box. Click **OK** to exit that box.

Click the **List Subjects** button at the bottom of the dialog box to see a partial list of newsgroup topics, like this:

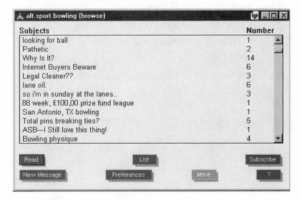

To read a message, click on it and then click the **Read** button near the bottom of the dialog box.

Posting a Message to a Newsgroup Using AOL

Suppose you now want to post a message to the bowling newsgroup. Click the **New Message** button at the bottom of the dialog box. This screen will appear:

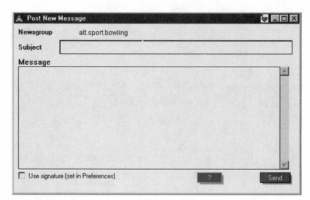

Type in your subject and your message and click the **Send** button. That's all there is to it!

Unsubscribing from a Newsgroup Using AOL

To cancel your subscription to the newsgroup (also called "unsubscribing"), return to the main AOL **Internet Newsgroups** dialog box. Click the **Read My Newsgroups** button. Highlight the name of the newsgroup that you want to cancel, click the **Remove** button at the bottom of the dialog box, and click **OK** to confirm the cancellation.

Newsgroup Etiquette ("Netiquette")

Newsgroup etiquette, sometimes called "Netiquette," is made up of a unique list of dos and don'ts dealing with online communication. As is the case with social etiquette, they touch on common courtesy, common sense, and personal safety. Following the rules of social etiquette, or of netiquette, just seems to make things run more smoothly for all. It is wise for you to review some of these rules before you begin participating in news groups.

- Do not, *under any circumstances*, post personal information (e.g., your telephone number or home address) on a newsgroup. You never can tell who might read that information. Common sense should reign supreme.

- Lurk before you leap. Visit the newsgroups that interest you a number of times before you begin posting messages on them. This will allow you to get a sense of the group and how its participants interact with one another. This approach—watching from the sidelines until you get "a sense of the game"—is commonly called "lurking."

- Read any FAQs (Frequently Asked Questions) you can locate. Most newsgroups have developed FAQs that cover important information for you to know. Reading the FAQs is a quick and easy way to begin to learn about a newsgroup.

- Post messages that are relevant to the topic. By reading the FAQs and lurking for a time, you should develop a sense of the types of questions that are appropriate and inappropriate for posting in the newsgroup.

- DON'T WRITE IN ALL CAPS. Typing messages in all caps is considered the electronic equivalent of shouting. It is frowned upon in postings.

- Alas, scams exist on the Internet, just as in the real world. If it sounds too good to be true, it is. In fact, if it sounds *almost* too good to be true, it probably is also.

Next Steps

Newsgroups are powerful Internet bulletin boards that allow you to connect and exchange information with others who share your interests. They can be a terrific source of information, whether you are interested in sports, travel, medical information, and much more.

Thousands and thousands of newsgroups are available on the Internet, and there are certain to be many on topics of immediate relevance to you. Your challenge, of course, is to locate the interesting or useful ones. It's worth the effort!

Chapter 8

Join Mailing Lists

In the introduction, I related the story of my wife's bout with breast cancer a few years ago. Much of the support we received at that time—both medical advice and emotional support—came from friends met only on the Internet.

Mailing Lists—The Great Equalizer

Soon after her diagnosis, my wife and I discovered and subscribed to a mailing list that was specifically for breast cancer patients and their partners. It consisted of nearly one thousand individuals: patients, a few physicians, and friends and partners of patients. As you can imagine, the participants' location, religion, social status, race, and political affiliation were of no concern to any of us. What we had in common was that we, or someone we cared about, was encountering breast cancer.

We e-mailed notes voicing our anxieties, concerns, questions, and dilemmas to a central computer housed we knew not where. That computer, called a "list server," in turn forwarded the e-mails to all other list subscribers. We responded to those messages when we felt we had something useful to say.

More commonly at that time, though, we would send questions to the list. Especially immediately following the diagnosis, we had a lot to learn and many decisions to make. Fortunately, no question was too simple or basic to be asked of others on the list. They had all been where we were and had all felt similar feelings.

I remember most clearly one note we posted. Given my wife's preliminary test results, the doctors were open to performing either a lumpectomy or a mastectomy. With subsequent treatment, the survival rates were virtually identical. It was her decision. So one evening I sent an e-mail to the list soliciting advice

from the voices of experience. I laid out her test results and what we understood the options to be. I asked others what they had decided in similar circumstances and why. I sent the e-mail late one night, shut off my computer, and went to bed.

By the time I logged on to the Internet the next morning, we had received no fewer than a dozen long, thoughtful responses from strangers from around the world. They shared their decisions regarding surgery, as well as their satisfactions and regrets regarding their decisions. Many of them stayed in touch with us by e-mail over the next many months, each of us following the other's progress as well as providing ongoing moral support.

Internet mailing lists are indeed a great equalizer of people, as well as an enormous source of support and information. Yet by no means are mailing lists all this serious.

Have you ever had one of those days when you wander around just baffled by a question regarding an obscure Old Icelandic tradition? Subscribe to Old Norse Net, whose goal is to provide a forum for discussion of problems regarding the medieval Scandinavian and North Atlantic societies. Are you interested in the biology of hydrothermal vents? Join the Deep Sea and Hydrothermal Vent Biology mailing list. There are mailing lists devoted to soccer coaching, medieval siege weaponry, and the Italian section of the American Folklore Society.

Name a topic, any topic. There is very likely to be an Internet mailing list devoted to it.

What Are Mailing Lists?

Conceptually, mailing lists are simple. They are much like the newsgroups you investigated in the previous chapter. You e-mail a question of interest to an Internet address (usually called a "list server" or "listserv"); others see your question and e-mail a response to you.

There are two general types of mailing lists, those that are moderated and those that are not. In moderated mailing lists, a person called the "moderator" reviews all messages (also called "postings"). That person decides which messages will be sent to the list subscribers.

Moderated lists often stay more clearly focused on the topic for which the list was designed. Also, in some lists, emotions and postings can become rather heated. A moderator can temper debate at such times.

Unmoderated lists are simply message clearinghouses. All other subscribers will see any message a subscriber posts to the list, regardless of its content.

Isn't This What Newsgroups Are For?

In newsgroups, messages are sent to the newsgroup, and you must go retrieve them there. With mailing lists, as the name implies, the list server receives all messages sent to the mailing list—comments, questions, and responses to questions—and then sends copies of all communications to *every* subscriber to the mailing list—you and the other four, four hundred, or four thousand individuals.

Does That Mean I Get a Lot of E-mail?

Generally there are two ways you can receive information from a mailing list. Either you can receive copies of *every* e-mail message posted to the group, or you can receive a "digest" version of the message exchanges. If you choose to receive copies of every communication, you might receive anywhere from one or two to two hundred (or more!) e-mail messages per day. The number depends upon how many subscribers there are and how many of them send e-mails to it in a given day. You might envision it like the illustration on the next page.

If you opt for the digest version, you still see all of the messages sent to the group, but they are all consolidated into one large e-mail document sent to you daily, if message volume warrants. Otherwise, the digests may come less frequently, but typically at least once a week.

How Do I Locate Mailing Lists That Interest Me?

As with other Internet tasks, this can be the biggest challenge. Unlike newsgroups, there is no complete, absolute repository that lists virtually all mailing lists in existence. L-Soft International, Inc. markets a list server product called LISTSERV that automates mailing list operations. As a service to Internet users, it also maintains a catalog of mailing lists open to the public.

Messages from the subscribers go to the list server.

The list server takes all the messages and forwards each one of them to you and to all other subscribers. This can result in *lots* of e-mail.

Copies of all messages come to you.

Mailing lists can send you lots of e-mail messages.

But consider the following: on December 2, 1998, L-Soft listed 20,572 public mailing lists. On December 3, 1998—one day later—that number had risen to 21,034. More than 400 new mailing lists came into existence in that 24-hour period! On December 6, 1998, that number had declined again to 20,979. Lists come and go. You can see how it might be difficult for you to sort through them all to find the mailing lists of interest to you.

So how do you find mailing lists of relevance to you? Often they are announced in newsgroups. Some are listed on Internet home pages. Some come by word of mouth (or by e-mail) from friends.

If you are interested in discovering a mailing list on a particular topic, you might begin by visiting L-Soft at

```
http://www.lsoft.com/lists/listref.html
```

You can use search tools at that website to locate mailing lists related to your topic of interest.

At that website you have a variety of options for locating mailing lists. You can, for example, click on **Search for a mailing list of interest**, and type a

Messages from the subscribers go to the list server.

The list server takes all the messages and consolidates them into one message called a "digest."

You receive just one, long e-mail message.

You can receive all of your mailing list e-mail messages as one consolidated list, called a "digest.",

keyword like "weather," "travel," "recipe," or "cancer." You will be shown a list of mailing lists that deal with that topic. You can click on any of the mailing lists to receive information on how to subscribe to that list.

There are other options on the main L-Soft website for searching for mailing lists. You can view mailing lists sorted by the country in which they are based. This is a good way to search for mailing lists if you are particularly interested in a specific country. You can also search for lists that have ten thousand or more subscribers (currently 152 lists) or those that have one thousand or more subscribers (currently 1,107).

How Do I Subscribe to a Mailing List?

Suppose you visit a webpage that deals with frombets, an obscure topic that has interested you for years, and find information about a frombet mailing list like that shown on the next page.

Subscribe to the Frombet News Summary

This FREE, weekly news summary includes abstracts of articles focusing on frombet technology that have recently appeared in major newspapers, magazines, and periodicals, as well as national and international wire services and websites... all in one convenient package.

To receive the Frombet News Summary via e-mail, just send an e-mail message containing only the line Subscribe FrombetNews FirstName LastName (there is no space between Frombet and News) to the address: listproc@frombetcity.com

If you happen to be a frombet collector or are interested in innovative frombet technology, you can subscribe to this mailing list by sending an e-mail message addressed to

`listproc@frombetcity.com`

If I were subscribing, the only line in my e-mail message would be

`Subscribe frombetnews Dan Fingerman`

Notice that capitalization is generally not important in this type of e-mail message:

`SUBSCRIBE FROMBETNEWS DAN FINGERMAN`

would work just as well.

How Do I Get a Digest Version of a Mailing List?

Soon after you subscribe to a mailing list, you will generally receive a welcome message in your e-mail. Since these welcome messages are generated automatically by computer, they will often appear in your e-mail inbox within only a few seconds of when you subscribe.

You should review the information in the message, as it often contains rules and protocol about using the list, together with information on how to receive a digest version of the list. It generally will also contain information on how to cancel your subscription to the list. You should save this message, either in the e-mail version or in print, for future reference.

For example, to receive the digest version of the frombet mailing list discussed earlier, the instructions might say to send this command: `set digests` to the list server. Whatever the command may be to receive a digest version of any given list, the instructions should be found in the list's initial welcome message.

What Other Commands Can I Use?

To have yourself removed from the list, you might need to send the command, `signoff frombet`. In contrast, if you are going to be on vacation for an extended period and do not want to receive e-mails from the mailing list during that time, you may be able to send the command, `set nomail` to turn off the e-mail or digests temporarily, without removing yourself from the mailing list entirely. Then, when you return from vacation, you send the command, `set mail`, and your mail resumes, just as before you left.

How Do I Send a Note that Goes to Everybody on the Mailing List?

There's a big difference between sending a command to the list server and sending a message that gets sent to everyone in the mailing list.

To send a message to all the people subscribed to the frombet list, you would send an e-mail to

```
news@frombetcity.com
```

This is called "sending mail to the list," because you send mail to a single address and the list server makes copies for all the people who have subscribed.

> (*) There is one address to which you send instructions to the list server regarding your subscription and another to which you send messages you want sent to everyone on the list. You should find out what those addresses are when you first subscribe to the list by carefully reading any confirming e-mail messages you receive after subscribing.

You should never send a command regarding your subscription (e.g., digest, nomail, etc.) to the mailing list distribution address, as it would be distributed to all subscribers. And besides, it wouldn't accomplish whatever it is you want it to do. In effect, you'd be "calling the wrong number."

> (*) **A Word of Warning: Never, never, never post identifying information like your address or telephone number on a mailing list. Alas, there are folks out there who will take advantage of that information in some nasty ways.**

Next Steps

Mailing lists are powerful Internet tools that allow you to connect and exchange information with others who share your interests using what are termed "cyber communities." If you have expertise on virtually any subject and are willing to share it with others, there is probably a mailing list in which you can do so. Conversely, if you are seeking information and advice on topics ranging from archeology to zoology, there is very likely to be a mailing list dealing with your topic of interest. Your task is to locate the mailing lists that interest you and subscribe and contribute to them for as long as you choose.

Go on out and explore what's there!

Chapter 9

Compute in Good Health

You have now mastered the basics of Internet exploration. You are familiar with the jargon, well-versed in Netiquette, and good at clicking. You have had the opportunity to see, firsthand, the mind-boggling diversity of information available to you on the Internet. You have begun to experiment with locating information of interest to you and navigating your way from this website to that one.

I hope you took me up on my invitation to send me an e-mail message at dan@typewritergeneration.com. I would certainly love to hear about some of your initial experiences using the Internet.*

However, before you continue to explore the Internet, I want to bring a few other important issues to your attention.

Computer Viruses

You may have heard reports on the local news warning of the havoc caused by computer viruses. Computer viruses are somewhat analogous to human viruses. Rather than being passed from person to person, they can be passed from computer to computer.

A computer virus is a small program that is created by a malicious programmer who might live next door to you or down the block or around the world. When this program runs on your computer, the results can range from annoying (a strange message appears on your screen) to disastrous (all of the information on your hard disk is destroyed).

Although viruses are extremely rare, you should be aware of the potential damage they can cause and of ways you can protect your computer.

---

*I regret that I am unlikely to be able to respond personally to most e-mail you send me. But rest assured, I will read all e-mail I receive.

How Could My Computer Get a Virus?

The good news is that virtually the only way your computer can get a virus is by running a program that contains that virus. The bad news is that there are files on the Internet that contain viruses. Should you happen to download one of these files onto your computer, your computer would likely become infected.

Computer virus infections can also be passed on diskettes that you might receive from other people. If a friend gives you a diskette that contains files, BEWARE! Be sure, at least, to ask your friend whether he or she has checked the disk for viruses before you put it into your computer.

Should I Do Anything To Protect My Computer?

There are two schools of thought when it comes to purchasing and using virus protection software. One school believes that since viruses and virus infections are so very rare, it is unnecessary to have virus protection software on your computer. They generally feel that if you exercise reasonable caution, i.e., you download files only from reputable websites and don't use diskettes that come from unfamiliar or unreliable sources, chances are good that you will never encounter a computer virus.

The other school of thought is that the purchase and the use of antivirus software is inexpensive insurance.

Every year I purchase homeowner's insurance. It has been a number of years since I last put in a claim on it. I continue to keep it in force, nonetheless. I also use antivirus software. Over the last fifteen years I have encountered really nasty computer viruses on only two or three occasions. But those encounters were sufficiently disruptive as to convince me to use antivirus software regularly.

How Do I Protect My Computer from Viruses?

Purchase, install, and use antivirus software. Update it regularly, according to the instructions that accompany it. Besides running the software as described in the manual, most current commercial antivirus software allows you to update it automatically over the Internet. You should do so as frequently as is recommended by the software company.

New viruses are created all the time. Each of the companies that produce the antivirus software listed below have staff whose job it is to identify, catalog, and figure out methods for dealing with new viruses. As new viruses come along, the antivirus software is modified so it can eliminate the new viruses. The antivirus software on your computer is only as good as the last time you updated it. If you are going to use it, you must get in the habit of updating your antivirus software regularly.

Where Do I Get Antivirus Software? What Software Should I Get?

Ask your computer mentor or computer-using friends where they suggest you purchase software. There are a few major commercial antivirus software products currently on the market, together with a number of smaller players.

The most widely used antivirus programs are:

- Norton AntiVirus, available from Symantec Corporation (`http://www.symantec.com`). This is the program I use, and have used for years. I find it easiest to use and highly reliable, *provided* you update the virus information on a very regular basis.

- McAfee VirusScan, Network Associates (`http://www.mcafee.com/`)

- Dr Solomon's Anti-Virus (`http://antivirus.drsolomon.com/`)

Not All Viruses Are Viruses: Beware of Hoaxes

You may from time to time receive e-mail messages from well-intentioned friends that read something like the following:

VIRUS WARNING!!!!!!!

If you receive an e-mail titled "JOIN THE CREW" DO NOT open it. It will erase everything on your hard drive. Forward this letter out to as many people as you can. This is a new, very malicious virus and not many people know about it. This information was announced yesterday morning from

IBM; please share it with everyone that might access the Internet. Once again, pass this along to EVERYONE in your address book so that this may be stopped. Also, do not open or even look at any mail that says "RE-TURNED OR UNABLE TO DELIVER." This virus will attach itself to your computer components and render them useless. Immediately delete any mail items that say this. AOL has said that this is a very dangerous virus and that there is NO remedy for it at this time. Please practice cautionary measures and forward this to all your online friends ASAP.

While viruses do indeed exist, many alerts that you might receive over e-mail, like this one, are hoaxes. Typically, this type of message is initiated by a prankster who enjoys seeing a fraudulent message spread far and wide.

There are a number of websites available that deal specifically with virus hoaxes. Before you ever forward a message containing a virus warning, you should always check at least one or more of the following websites to determine whether the warning you have received is a hoax.

- Symantec AntiVirus Research Center (`http://www.symantec.com/avcenter/hoax.html`)

- Computer Incident Advisory Capability (CAIC), a division of the United States Department of Energy (`http://ciac.llnl.gov/ciac/CIACHoaxes.html`)

- Computer Virus Myths (`http://www.kumite.com/myths/home.htm`)

If the website indicates that the information you have received is a hoax and you know the person who sent it to you, you should write back to that person and alert them to the hoax. Then you should simply delete the e-mail message from your inbox and not forward it to anyone else.

Compute in Comfort—You Deserve It!

Be warned: computing can be dangerous to your health. As you explore the Internet more, you may find that you begin to develop aches and pains in parts of your body that were formerly fine. Some of the common culprits include the following:

- Staring up at a monitor over an extended period can lead to headaches, eye strain, and neck or shoulder pain.

- Typing on the keyboard and using a mouse can lead to finger, hand, wrist, elbow, and shoulder pains.

- Sitting at your computer in an uncomfortable chair can result in neck, shoulder, back, and leg pain.

Fortunately, a few precautions can help prevent these potential problems.

Your Monitor

To some degree, common sense rules. Sitting too close to your monitor can lead to eye strain. Sitting too far away can make it difficult to read small text. If your monitor is higher or lower than your eye level, it puts additional stress either on your neck or on your eyes, by forcing you to look upward or downward for extended periods.

Some solutions to consider:

- There are commercially available computer desks that have platforms designed to hold your monitor at approximately eye level.

- Many companies (you can search for them on the Web!) sell adjustable monitor stands that can raise or lower your monitor to a level comfortable for you.

- I suggest, before you invest in either of the previous two solutions, you experiment with monitor height by using the time-honored technique of placing one or more out-of-date telephone books under your monitor until you determine what monitor height is the most comfortable for you to use. Then you can find a more aesthetically pleasing product to serve the same function.

- You should also place your monitor carefully, with respect to win-

dows in your room. Positioning it directly in front of a window can cause eyestrain by having the relatively dim image on your screen surrounded by bright outside light. Having a window behind you when you are at your computer can cause reflected glare on your screen. The ideal position is to have windows in your room on your left or right, so light from them is not reflected into your eyes.

- When you get your computer, you should also experiment with the image controls that are usually placed on the front of the monitor, below the screen. In particular, you can adjust the brightness of the display so it is most comfortable for you to look at.

Your Keyboard and Mouse

How frequently have you used a typewriter over the last decade or two? While some of you might say "often," many of you have probably used a typewriter infrequently, if at all. So it will come as no surprise to most of you that using your computer keyboard a great deal as you begin to investigate the Internet can put stress on little-used muscles in your hands, arms, and shoulders. Similarly, sliding a mouse around on the desktop next to your keyboard can put unaccustomed stress on these muscles.

The *American Heritage Dictionary* defines "ergonomics" as "The applied science of equipment design, as for the workplace, intended to maximize productivity by reducing operator fatigue and discomfort." Fortunately, many companies have created ergonomic devices that can make your computer use far more comfortable. Virtually all such devices can be found at numerous websites on the Internet. Use your favorite search engine and try searching jointly for terms such as "computer" and "ergonomic."

Some solutions to consider:

- There are a number of ergonomically designed keyboards commercially available. Rather than having all of the keys laid out in straight lines, as you might be used to on a typewriter, many of the keyboards divide the keys vertically, roughly in the middle, and rotate each half slightly outward so that your hands can rest on the keyboard in a more natural, relaxed manner. For many years, I have used the Microsoft Natural Keyboard, which I find quite comfortable for extended typing.

If you use your favorite search engine, and the keywords "ergonomic" and "keyboard," you will find any number of websites where you can look at ergonomically designed keyboards.

- If it is uncomfortable for you to use your keyboard in a normal position, you might want to investigate wireless keyboards that you can rest in your lap and type on at some distance away from your computer.

- There is no doubt that for most people using a mouse with the computer makes investigating the Internet far easier. But computer mice and related input devices come in various shapes, sizes, and types. If you find that using the mouse that came with your computer is uncomfortable, a visit to your local computer emporium might be in order. Most large computer stores carry a variety of mice and related input devices that you can actually try before you buy.

  Besides mice, you should also investigate and try input devices called "track balls" which serve the same function as mice but stay in one position on your desk. You move the cursor around on your screen by manipulating a ball, usually using your thumb or other fingers to rotate it in its housing.

  Many years ago, I developed tendonitis in my right elbow while writing my first book. The mouse I was using at the time simply was not a good one for me. At that time, I told all of my friends and colleagues that I had developed "tennis elbow," thinking that the term was somehow more elegant and socially acceptable than "mouse elbow." Since then, I have used and very much liked a series of track balls produced by Logitech (`http://www.logitech.com`).

- If you are left-handed, you should know that you can reverse the buttons on a standard mouse so that you can use your left hand in

the same manner as most of us use our right hands for the mouse. Either ask your computer mentor how to switch the buttons or, if necessary, investigate the mouse settings in your computer's **Control Panel**. You access the **Control Panel** by clicking on the **Start** button on your screen and then choosing **Settings**, followed by **Control Panel**. Double-click the **Mouse** icon in the screen that appears. You will need to investigate the options in the **Mouse** dialog box, as each mouse has a different layout of controls.

- Another alternative for left-handers is to purchase a mouse that is ergonomically designed for a left hand.

- If using the keyboard is either a daunting task, or is impossible for you due to physical limitations, consider investigating speech recognition software. Controlling computers by voice has been a long-sought goal in this industry. In fact, if you have a reasonably new and powerful computer, software does now exist that allows you to speak into a microphone and have your words appear in type on your screen.

  About ten percent of this book, for example, was dictated into a microphone on my headset and then transcribed by my computer. I have been working with and training this software for about two months now, and its transcription accuracy is now on the order of ninety-five percent. The software does tend to confuse words that sound identical, like "to", "too," and "two," as well as words that sound very similar to one another.

  A number of companies produce speech recognition software. Before you purchase such a program, you should read as much as you can about it in computer publications and, if possible, get recommendations from friends. The program I use and find to be quite powerful and accurate is called Dragon NaturallySpeaking. You can find information about it at `http://www.dragonsys.com`. The other major speech recognition software product is IBM ViaVoice (`http://www.software.ibm.com/speech/`).

Furniture

Your monitor desk and your chair combine to control both the distance and angle from which you view your screen. Consider them both as you begin to use your computer more frequently. There are a wide variety of commercial computer desks available that are designed to hold your monitor at a comfortable eye level and often have a shelf or drawer for your keyboard and mouse so they are at a level most comfortable for your arms. Again, investigate the Internet and visit stores near you. Look at the kinds of computer desks your friends and neighbors use for their Internet browsing, see what you like and don't like about their set-ups and get new ideas from them.

There are also a variety of hi-tech chairs available over a wide range of prices. Try searching out "ergonomic" and "chairs" on the Internet. You will find many options in all price ranges.

Next Steps

My intent in writing this book was to introduce you to the amazing array of information and choices provided by the Internet. More importantly, I wanted to whet your appetite so you continue to explore and expand your Internet horizons.

Thus far you have only glimpsed the tip of the Internet iceberg. Now go ahead and find information that is of relevance and of immediate use to you. Find answers to important questions you might have on health, finances, travel, religion, or politics. Also, indulge your sense of whimsy. Locate sites that make you laugh or otherwise brighten your day. Pass them along to others. Connect in new ways with family and friends. Share your knowledge freely and gain from the knowledges of others.

Indeed, the times, they are a changin'. The world and the universe are out there for you to explore in entirely new ways. Take advantage of the new technology to which you now have access. Explore, learn, share, connect, and enrich your life in whole new ways.

May your journey onto the Internet be a wonderful one!

Chapter 10

A Wealth of Websites

Over the years, as well as in the process of researching this book, I have found numerous websites, books, and journal articles that list topic areas of interest to numbers of the "typewriter generation." In this chapter, I list and briefly describe a number of websites, broken down by general topic areas. I have also exercised my writer's license to insert some whimsical categories of my own.

There are two reasons for including this chapter in the book. First, of course, I want to point out to you Internet locations that I think you might find interesting. Also, and more importantly, I want you to see a sample of the incredible diversity of information to which you now have access. I suggest you browse through this chapter with a pen, pencil, or highlighter in hand. Mark those websites that might be of interest to you. Then go visit them on the Internet!

Accumulating the information in this chapter spanned roughly six months, not counting the websites I had previously discovered. By the time I finished writing, some of the information in this chapter was already out of date! More of it will become outdated by the time you read these words. Websites come and websites go. That is the way of the Internet world.

To visit any of the following websites, remember that you must type the website address (the URL) *exactly* as shown, excluding parentheses surrounding it. For example, to go to the Grateful Med (`http://igm.nlm.nih.gov/`) medical information database at the National Library of Medicine, you must type:

```
http://igm.nlm.nih.gov/
```

with the spelling exactly as shown here. Be careful when you type not to substitute the letter "O" for the number "0" (zero) and use capital letters where in-

dicated. For those of you who grew up using a typewriter, no longer can you substitute a lower-case letter "l" for the number "1" (one). As smart as computers are, they are quite unforgiving of typing errors.

Think back to Chapter 3 in which you began to explore connecting to websites. You may remember that you experimented with typing in only the "core" part of web addresses, omitting the "http://".

For example, if you want to visit `http://www.cnn.com`, you should experiment with just typing cnn and pressing ENTER . Your browser will likely complete the typing of the rest of the URL for you and contact the website with little effort on your part.

If you experiment with this technique, you will find you'll do more and type less. Less typing means a lower likelihood of typing mistakes, corrections, and unnecessary keystrokes. Here is a case where keeping things simple means making life easier and better.

If you can't get to one of the websites listed, first check your typing and correct any mistakes you might have made. If you still can't access a website, it may have ceased to exist between the time I wrote this and the time you're reading it. Try finding similar websites, using the search techniques you practiced in Chapter 5.

With the sole exception of `http://www.typewritergeneration.com`, *inclusion of a listing in this chapter should not be viewed as an endorsement by the author nor the publisher of any organization, product, nor information offered on the website.* I encourage you to begin your browsing at what I consider to be perhaps the most important (if not necessarily the most useful) website on the Internet.

The Internet for the Typewriter Generation

`http://www.typewritergeneration.com`
Come visit the only website on the Internet based on this book! You will find links to all of the websites listed in the rest of this chapter, updated as appropriate. Also, you might just find some of your author's musings on interesting websites and information I have found in my Internet wanderings. Finally, feel free to e-mail

me interesting websites you have discovered. Send them to me at `dan@typewritergeneration.com` and you might be surprised to find them added to my list of links and perhaps even included in a revision of this book! Share your knowledge and your discoveries. That, after all, is what the Internet is all about.

News

Broadcast News

CNN
(`http://cnn.com/`)
If you like CNN on your television, this website should make you feel right at home on the Internet. It is updated frequently as news breaks throughout the day. You can find not only news here, but also weather, current business and stock market information, book reviews, and information on such topics as health and travel. You can also customize your CNN news page so it highlights news stories that are of greatest interest to you.

ABC News
(`http://www.abcnews.com`)
Yet another way to get breaking news at any time, day or night. You can also create a custom news page that includes local news throughout the United States.

CBS News
(`http://www.cbs.com`)
If you prefer CBS coverage of the news, this is the website to visit for news and, as they say on television, "much, much more." You can find the local weather forecast, sports scores, and information on local CBS-affiliate stations at this website.

MSNBC
(`http://www.msnbc.com/`)
This collaborative site between Microsoft and NBC brings you news, general information, and editorial opinions from MSNBC, NBC, the Associated Press, Reuters, and other sources.

Print News

The New York Times
(`http://www.nytimes.com/`)
The *New York Times* on the Internet provides the full content of today's print edition, together with breaking news updates from the Associated Press and special columns written specifically for the website. It also gives you access to the archived *Times* information, as well as other features.

The Times of London
(`http://www.the-times.co.uk/`)
View the world and its news from the perspective of this venerable source. The *Times* and the *Sunday Times* are published here, as well as the *Times Literary Supplement*, the *Times Educational Supplement*, and the *Times Higher Education Supplement*. To view the site, you must register a username for yourself, as well as specify a password. Registration is free at the time of this writing.

The Washington Post
(`http://www.washingtonpost.com/`)
From where a lot of news is made, the Internet-based version of the *Washington Post* includes front-page news, as well as a selection of business news, international and national news, sports, style, Washington World, weather, opinion, and classified ads.

Wall Street Journal
(`http://www.wsj.com/`)
This website provides some information from the *Wall Street Journal* that anyone can access. For complete access to all of the features of the site, as well as access to Barron's Online, you must purchase an annual subscription. There is information for subscribing at the website.

The Financial Times
(`http://www.ft.com/`)
Get direct access to this famous international business newspaper.

Newspapers Online
(http://www.newspapers.com/)
Are you particularly interested in how the world is viewed from the vantage point of Bhutan or Bahrain, Singapore or Slovenia? This site contains links both to newspapers in the United States and around the world, sorted by country. It also has links to trade journals, specialty publications (did you know that Deary, Idaho, pop. 580, has its own newspaper on the Internet that reports on the lifestyle and events of the region?), college and university newspapers, and religious publications.

Select Ware News
(http://www.select-ware.com/news/)
Here is another site that links you to hundreds of newspapers and newswires around the world. The sites are broken down by country, with newspaper links available in each country listed on the screen. A fascinating site for those of us interested in travel and how the world views the news.

The Drudge Report
(http://www.drudgereport.com/)
Whether or not you agree with Matt Drudge's reporting style, his website is a fascinating one to investigate. Here you will find links to your favorite (and least favorite) syndicated columnists, as well as to an eclectic set of news sources as diverse as the Associated Press, United Press International, the *Christian Science Monitor*, the *National Enquirer*, *North Korean News*, the *Islamic Wire of Iran*, and the *Jewish World Review*.

Sports News

CBS Sportsline
(http://cbs.sportsline.com)
Come here for the latest professional and college sports scores, live sports radio, women's and world sports results, information on sports superstars, as well as announcements of sports jobs and information on health, fitness, and recre-

ational sports. You can also come here to read feature columns, view still photos and video, and hear audio reports from sports around the world.

Women's Sports Network
(http://womenoutside.com/)
The Women's Sports Network offers scores, equipment reviews, schedules and events, and player profiles for professional, Olympic, and high-school sports.

AllSports
(http://www.allsports.com/)
The NFL, NHL, NBA, major league baseball, NASCAR, the Olympics, cricket, and soccer. Come by this website for information and scores on all of these.

CNN/Sports Illustrated
(http://www.cnnsi.com/)
Come visit this powerful sports reporting team. Currently, this website covers U.S. baseball, professional and college football and basketball, hockey, golf, tennis, soccer, motor sports, and women's sports. Scores, articles, audio and video reports, and news are all here.

ESPN SportsZone
(http://espn.go.com/)
Drop by this sports powerhouse to learn about college and professional sports with ESPN radio and television sports news.

SportsNews
(http://www.worldwidenews.com/moresp.htm)
SportsNews is a one-stop shopping center for links to sports news sources around the world. If it's happening somewhere in the sports world, chances are pretty good that you can find a link to whatever "it" is here at SportsNews.

Travel
Local Information/Getting Around

If you're going to San Francisco (or practically anywhere else) and are disinclined to wear flowers in your hair, perhaps you should visit one of these sites to see what is happening in the destination city of your choice.

Microsoft Sidewalk
(`http://national.sidewalk.msn.com/`)
At the time this is being written, Sidewalk provides access to yellow pages, a buyer's guide, and entertainment information for approximately seventy-five cities around the United States. In most of these cities you can find at which theaters movies are showing, see new (or favorite) restaurants, and find a winery, beach, street fair, sports event, or museum to visit. You can also personalize Sidewalk so when a particular performer or sports team is coming to town or a certain type of event is happening locally, you will be notified automatically by e-mail.

Citysearch
(`http://citysearch.com/`)
Currently citysearch contains a wide variety of information on more than a dozen cities in the United States, as well as Melbourne, Sydney, Toronto, Stockholm, and Copenhagen. For example, the San Francisco page includes sections on art galleries, books, lectures, kids' and family activities, movies, museums, nightlife, and theater. It also lists bars and restaurants, both college and professional sports, events, and hotels. It also contains links to surrounding areas.

Mapquest
(`http://www.mapquest.com/`)
Are you going to be visiting Minneapolis and need a map of the area around 8th Street and Hennepin Avenue? Perhaps you're staying with friends near 50th

and France Avenue and need driving instructions to the Humphrey Metrodome to catch a Minnesota Vikings football game. Whether it's a map of a locale or detailed driving directions from here to there, a quick visit to Mapquest will get you the information you need.

Travels Taking you a Little Farther?

Microsoft Expedia
(http://expedia.msn.com/)
Search for low air fares, purchase tickets, reserve a hotel room or a car, investigate cruises, discover last-minute travel bargains, all without lifting a telephone to call a travel agent.

Travelocity
(http://travelocity.com/)
Like Expedia, Travelocity also lets you locate low air fares and reserve rental cars and hotel rooms. They also have listings of over twenty thousand bed and breakfast facilities, discount fares, and "fare watcher e-mail ," a service in which you can specify up to five round-trip itineraries and Travelocity will send you an e-mail whenever the fares change.

Fodor's
(http://www.fodors.com/)
While you can use Fodor's site in much the same way as Expedia and Travelocity, Fodor's uses its vast international experience to expand the travel information available to you. Whether your travels are going to take you to Jerusalem or Singapore, Helsinki or Hong Kong, this is a website to visit. For any of nearly one hundred destinations, you can request a "miniguide" that covers local tourist sites, hotels, restaurants of all sorts, currency, tipping protocol, public transit, and much more. What a wonderful way to get a quick overview of your destination!

Lonely Planet
(http://www.lonelyplanet.com/)
In the spirit of the Lonely Planet travel guidebooks, this slightly irreverent site provides you with literally a world of information associated with travel. If you have browsed and liked their books, you'll love this site. The site also contains an eclectic collection of links to other travel-related websites. Link topics include such basics as packing tips and visa and health information to more obscure topics such as offbeat travel, eco-travel, and worldwide festivals.

Great Outdoor Recreation Pages
(http://www.gorp.com/)
This website is designed for travelers who tend to want to go and see and do, rather than go and relax. There are feature articles here, as well as a listing of interesting travel opportunities, broken down by type of activity, ranging from hiking and biking to birding, snorkeling, off-road driving, and hang gliding. It is an extremely varied site, containing a wide variety of information designed to get you thinking about your next trip.

Special Travel Needs?

Society for the Advancement of Travel for the Handicapped
(http://www.sath.org)
This site contains travel tips for people who have special needs, as well as links to a variety of travel resources serving this population.

Access-Able
(http://www.access-able.com)
This website is designed to provide "access information to mature and disabled travelers." The site contains FAQs, information on accessible cruise lines, and listings of travel agencies that plan trips for people with special needs. It also has forums and a bulletin board on which you can share your experiences, ask questions, and get advice. It also has lists of accessible lodging and tourist at-

tractions worldwide, access guides, and information on van and equipment rental and repair. There are also a variety of useful links.

Weather and Related Information

Most of the news websites, including those of CNN, MSNBC, CBS, and ABC, have links that will display your local weather forecast. But for detailed information, check out the following sites.

The National Weather Service
(`http://www.nws.noaa.gov/`)
Go to the source. This site is a service of the U.S. National Oceanic and Atmospheric Administration (NOAA). It has not only current and forecasted conditions throughout the United States, but also historical and statistical weather data available to anyone interested in weather research. For example, did you know that the mean temperature in January in Barter Island, Alaska, is -13.1°F?

The Weather Channel
(`http://www.weather.com/`)
Whether it is the local weather you want or Doppler radar and satellite animations like you see on the eleven o'clock news, it's all here, together with specific information like skiers' or golfers' weather.

AccuWeather
(`http://www.accuweather.com/`)
"The World's Weather Leader", this site provides forecasts by location and by what they term "product" (hurricane, precipitation, radar, recreation, satellites, etc.). You can also register to have them send you daily e-mail messages containing the weather forecast for your area. At the time of this writing, this service is free, although there is a notice on the site that they may apply a small subscription fee for this service in the future.

BBC Weather Centre
(http://www.bbc.co.uk/weather/)
Here is a weather website that focuses on the United Kingdom. It has the U.K. broken down by thirteen regions, so you can easily find out the forecast for the southwestern coast, Edinburgh, or Leeds.

U.S. Geological Survey
(http://www.usgs.gov/)
If you, like me, live in a seismically active area or are interested in other geological topics, you might like to see up-to-the-hour information on the USGS website. Information on earthquakes, wildfires, landslides, and other such phenomena are available here.

You might want to check from time to time to see how recently the author was awakened by a 3.0+ on the Richter scale. For those of you so inclined, you can follow Northern California and Nevada seismic activity at

```
http://quake.wr.usgs.gov/recenteqs/
```

Or, for information on Northern California only,

```
http://www.scecdc.scec.org/recenteqs/Maps/122-38.html
```

Health/Medical Websites

While writing this book, I received an e-mail that was circulating on the Internet that reported a supposed correlation between a widely used artificial sweetener and certain serious medical conditions. It quoted research reports and medical experts from around the world. Within a day of receiving the original report, it was denounced on a nationally syndicated radio medical talk program, and a few days later I received another e-mail indicating that the previous one contained completely erroneous information.

To some degree, common sense rules here. Seek and trust medical information from websites sponsored by reputable medical organizations. If you receive e-mail regarding a newly discovered, wonderful cure for X, beware. If sci-

ence discovers a wonderful cure for a disease, you are probably not likely to read about it in a secret message on the Internet. More likely it will make front-page headlines in your newspaper.

It is important to recognize that the websites shown below, as well as others you might locate on your own, can at best offer only general advice about a medical condition. *It is essential that you use these websites to supplement, not replace, information you receive from your own medical advisors. Note that inclusion of a listing in this section should not be viewed as an endorsement by the author nor the publisher of any organization, product, nor information offered on the website.*

General Medical Information, Research, and Wellness

Grateful Med
(http://igm.nlm.nih.gov/)
This website, sponsored by the National Library of Medicine at the National Institutes of Health, allows you to search for abstracts of recent articles that have appeared in nearly four thousand medical journals worldwide. The MEDLINE bibliographic database incorporates article abstracts in medicine, nursing, dentistry, veterinary medicine, and the health-care system.

Mayo Clinic Health Oasis
(http://www.mayohealth.org/)
This excellent website of general information and links is based at the world-famous Mayo Clinic in Minnesota. Its information is current, useful, and highly readable. It includes medical tips, quizzes designed to test your knowledge of various conditions, reference articles, first aid information, and links to other sites on the Internet.

Your Health Daily
(http://yourhealthdaily.com)
This site contains "timely, in-depth articles on a variety of health news topics, written for general readers and health professionals." These are well-written articles by professional journalists.

WellnessWeb Senior's Center
(`http://wellweb.com/SENIORS/ELDERSHP.HTM`)
WellnessWeb describes itself as "a collaboration of patients, health-care professionals, and other caregivers. [Its] mission is to help you find the best and most appropriate medical information and support available. You'll find information about clinical trials, community health, drug dosages and compliance, treatment options and research, how to select a health-care provider, reports on dozens of illnesses and conditions, tips about healthy lifestyles, complementary treatment alternatives and options, and many more topics."

Note that in the section entitled "How Do We Financially Support WellnessWeb?" they indicate that "To help us continue to offer the highest quality information that is in the best interests of patients and consumers, we will accept selective sponsorships and educational grants from health-care and other companies to help them create awareness about their products."

Such full disclosure is a plus, but common sense consumerism suggests you keep in mind the sponsorship when viewing information on the site.

HealthCentral
(`http://www.healthcentral.com/`)
Perhaps you've heard him on his syndicated radio talk show or seen him on television. At this site you can find out the latest general health information from Dr. Dean Edell.

Allergies

Pollen Forecasts Throughout the United States
(`http://www.allegra.com/pollenframe.htm`)
This service is sponsored by Hoechst Marion Roussel USA, the manufacturers of the antihistamine, Allegra. When I travel, I always like to be forewarned about the pollen level at my destination. This site allows me to do so.

Maps of Pollen in the United States
(`http://CNN.com/WEATHER/allergy/index.html`)
A service of CNN Interactive, this is part of the CNN Weather website.

Alzheimer's Disease

Alzheimer's Association
(`http://www.alz.org/`)
According to information on this website, Alzheimer's disease is a progressive, degenerative disease of the brain and the most common form of dementia. It currently affects approximately 4 million Americans. In 1993, approximately 19 million Americans said they had a family member with Alzheimer's, and 37 million knew someone with the disease.

This website gives you information on the disease, as well as information on medical issues, research, and caregiving.

The Alzheimer's Page
(`http://www.biostat.wustl.edu/alzheimer/`)
The Alzheimer's Page is an educational service created and sponsored by the Washington University Alzheimer's Disease Research Center in St. Louis, Missouri. It is supported, in part, by a grant from the National Institute on Aging.

It contains frequently asked questions (with answers), as well as a variety of other information about the disease.

Alzheimer's Support Network
(`http://gator.naples.net/presents/Alzheimer/alinks.html`)
This site has no specific information of its own, but contains a large number of links to other Alzheimer's-related sites.

Cancer

American Cancer Society
(http://www.cancer.org/)
This page contains information and current news on cancer.

CancerNet
(http://cancernet.nci.nih.gov/)
This site is a service of the National Cancer Institute, a component of the United States National Institutes of Health. It contains various information based on current research designed for patients, medical professionals, and researchers. The information comes from PDQ, the National Cancer Institute's cancer database, which includes summaries on current cancer treatments, screening, prevention, supportive care, and ongoing clinical trials.

It also contains links to a wide variety of other cancer-related websites.

Breast Cancer Information
(http://www.breastcancerinfo.com/)
Sponsored by the Susan G. Komen Breast Cancer Foundation, which is "dedicated to eradicate breast cancer as a life-threatening disease by advancing research, education, screening, and treatment."

Prostate Cancer Information
(http://www.prostateinfocenter.com/)
This website is sponsored by the pharmaceutical company, Hoechst Marion Roussel, USA. It provides general information and web referrals to other resources for the estimated 300,000 men each year who are diagnosed with this disease.

Diabetes

CDC's Diabetes and Public Health Resource
(http://www.cdc.gov/nccdphp/ddt/ddthome.htm)
According to the information on this website, almost 16 million Americans

have diabetes, but about one-third of them are not aware of their condition. Produced by the Centers for Disease Control and Prevention, this website provides a wealth of information on diabetes. This particular division "translates scientific research findings into health promotion, disease prevention, and treatment strategies." It contains a section of frequently asked questions (FAQs) about diabetes.

The Diabetes Monitor
(`http://www.mdcc.com/`)
This website monitors diabetes developments that are published on the Internet. Through its Diabetes Registry, it has links to websites that deal with a wide range of diabetes-related issues, such as governmental issues on diabetes and traveling with diabetes. It's "Diabetes on the Web" section contains a "hodgepodge of hyperlinks to huge and humble homepages, websites, and web pages that have information (sometimes very useful, and sometimes not) about diabetes and related health issues."

Headache/Migraine

The Journal of the American Medical Association
Migraine Information Center
(`http://www.ama-assn.org/special/migraine/migraine.htm`)
Find out the latest news, research results, and treatments for migraine headaches. There is also an education and support center here, containing resources both for patients and medical professionals, as well as a list of hyperlinks to related websites.

National Headache Foundation
(`http://www.headaches.org/`)
This website discusses a broad range of headache symptoms, medications, and treatments in an effort to inform and educate visitors. It contains educational materials, information on a variety of headache topics, referrals to support groups, and breaking news stories on this topic.

MAGNUM: Migraine Awareness Group:
A National Understanding for Migraineurs
(http://www.migraines.org/)
This organization was created to "bring public awareness, utilizing the electronic, print, and artistic mediums, to the fact that Migraine is a true organic neurological disease." It includes news about migraines, migraine myths and reality, treatments and management, where to turn for help, and FAQs.

Heart Disease

American Heart Association
(http://www.amhrt.org)
The American Heart Association is "dedicated to providing you with education and information on fighting heart disease and stroke." It contains information on warning signs and risk assessment, family health, heart diseases, conditions, and treatments; stroke prevention; and treatment and recovery for non-healthcare professionals. It also has publications, research, and statistics for science and medical professionals, as well as news coverage on recent relevant developments.

Heart Care Network
(http://www.merck.com/pro/hcn/)
"The Heart Care Network is an alliance of general practitioners, cardiologists, and internists who share a common goal: to improve the quality of treatment for coronary heart disease patients in hospital and community settings." Merck & Co., Inc. sponsors this website, which contains a variety of information about heart disease, as well as links to other organizations that deal with heart care.

High Blood Pressure/Hypertension

Controlling High Blood Pressure: A Woman's Guide
(http://www.nih.gov/health/hbp/index.htm)
This guide is part of a public health collaboration of The Alliance for Aging

Research; the National Heart, Lung, and Blood Institute; and the National Institutes of Health. This guide teaches how blood pressure can be controlled through a combination of diet, exercise, and medications.

Hypertension Network
(http://www.bloodpressure.com/)
The mission of this organization is "to improve the quality of care of people suffering from high blood pressure by helping them get information about this common medical condition which affects 50 million Americans and find physicians with a special interest and expertise in treating them. We provide weekly updates of new research findings and recommendations of interest to people with hypertension, written exclusively by physicians and nurses who are experts in the field, and in clear non-technical language."

Osteoporosis

National Osteoporosis Foundation
(http://www.nof.org/)
This is a source of information on causes, prevention, detection, and treatment of osteoporosis. It contains information for both patients and professionals, as well as links to support groups and reports on the most recent medical and political information related to this condition.

Osteoporosis and Related Bone Diseases~National Resource Center
(http://www.osteo.org/)
Osteoporosis is a major public health threat for 28 million Americans, eighty percent of whom are women. In the U.S. today, 10 million individuals already have osteoporosis and 18 million more have low bone mass, placing them at increased risk for this disease. One out of every two women and one in eight men over fifty will have an osteoporosis-related fracture in their lifetime.

This site contains news and research about osteoporosis, as well as links to related sites.

National Institute of Arthritis and Musculoskeletal and Skin Diseases
(http://www.nih.gov/niams/)
This division of the National Institutes of Health conducts and supports research on a wide variety of diseases. It is also a source for recent news on related areas.

Pain Management

American Academy of Pain Management
(http://www.aapainmanage.org/)
The American Academy of Pain Management is the largest multidisciplinary pain society and largest physician-based pain society in the United States. The website provides information for professionals and for patients needing pain management assistance. It has a directory of pain management programs around the world, as well as a number of links to other related sites.

Worldwide Congress on Pain
(http://www.pain.com/)
This website contains news and information on pain management and related topics. News reports appear to be updated regularly, and there are links to both United States and international pain societies and associations, foundations and organizations, pain publications, pain studies, and libraries, as well as a variety of other related health resources. There are also chat rooms in which you can post a question or concern and others can respond to you.

OncoLink: Pain Management
(http://oncolink.upenn.edu/specialty/pain/)
Sponsored by the University of Pennsylvania Cancer Center, this site contains pain-related information, especially, but not exclusively, related to cancer. An unusual and especially useful feature of this site is that it has compiled a list of Internet-wide e-mail discussion groups, called "listservers," to which you can subscribe. When you subscribe to these groups, you will receive frequent e-mails on topics of interest to you. (Refer to Chapter 8 for more information on this type of group.)

Stroke

National Stroke Association
(http://www.stroke.org/)
The stated goal of this association is "reducing the incidence and impact of stroke." It has a variety of basic information on stroke, as well as survivor and caregiver resources, prevention programs, and links to related websites.

National Institute of Neurological Disorders and Stroke
(http://www.ninds.nih.gov/)
Part of the National Institutes of Health, under the U.S. Department of Health and Human Services, this site contains information about cutting-edge scientific discoveries as well as more general information on stoke and other neurological disorders, including epilepsy and Parkinson's disease.

Stroke and Cerebrovascular Disease:
A Guide for Patients and Their Families
(http://www.med.stanford.edu/school/stroke/)
This valuable site, presented by the Stanford Stroke Center at the Stanford University Medical Center, is in two sections. Part one deals with the different types of stroke, describes the warning signs and risk factors for stroke, and recommends steps you can take to reduce your risk for stroke. Part two provides an overview of the advanced techniques for diagnosis and treatment available at the Stanford Stroke Center.

Elder Care

According to U.S. Census Bureau statistics, the average lifespan in 1900 in the United States was 46.3 years for men and 48.3 years for women. In 1950, those numbers changed to 65.6 years for men and 71.1 years for women. As we approach the end of this century, men live to an average age of 72 years, and women to 79 years. As more of us live longer, there are more and more resources designed to meet our needs, including resources on the Internet.

The Resource Directory for Older People
(http://www.aoa.dhhs.gov/aoa/dir/77.html)
This site is a cooperative effort of the National Institute on Aging and the Administration on Aging. Its mission statement reads, "Children of Aging Parents (CAPS) is a nonprofit organization that provides information and emotional support to caregivers of older people. CAPS serves as a national clearinghouse for information on resources and issues dealing with older people."

The National Institute on Aging
(http://www.nih.gov/nia/)
NIA is a U.S. government-sponsored agency that conducts and supports biomedical, social, and behavioral research and public education. It reports news and research results on aging.

Careguide
(http://www.eldercare.com/)
This website provides links to elder-care sites with topics like nursing homes, assisted living, home care, hospice, and care managers in over 5,000 cities throughout the United States. It also has resources including articles on how to determine if your parents need assistance, long distance caregiving, and a variety of similar topics.

Children of Aging Parents
(http://www.careguide.net/g.cgi?/careguide.cgi/caps/
capshome.htm!^Alliances_CAPS_textlink^index.htm!)
This nonprofit organization's website provides information and referrals, educational outreach, support groups and a speakers bureau on topics relating to aging.

Extended Care Information Network
(http://www.elderconnect.com/Eldercare/public/main.html)
If you or someone you love can no longer live without assistance, whether because of illness, disability, or for some other reason, this site offers extremely useful information ranging from assessing your loved one's needs to choosing

from among services such as adult day care, assisted living, home health-care options, hospice, intermediate care facilities, nursing homes, respite care, retirement communities, and skilled or subacute care.

When you're faced with having to make difficult decisions, websites like this one can provide you with a wealth of information.

Religion

Sites listed below are intended to be illustrative of the quantity and diversity of religious information available on the Internet. The list is by no means an exhaustive collection of religions, denominations, or religious web pages.

Catholic

Catholic Information Center on Internet
(http://www.catholic.net/)
This site contains links to the latest news from Catholic World News, as well as a variety of information ranging from Papal Encyclicals to information on Pope John Paul II, liturgy, and a church locator. It also contains movie reviews produced by the National Conference of Catholic Bishops.

Catholic Online
(http://www.catholic.org/)
Catholic Online says it is the most comprehensive Catholic information service available on the Internet. "The mission of Catholic Online is to serve as a center for the exchange of information for Catholics and all people of God, to help them deepen their understanding of our Catholic faith." It contains daily news, specifically Catholic news, searchable information on saints, as well as a marketplace specializing in Catholic software, religious articles, tours, etc.

The Vatican
(http://www.vatican.va/)
Go to the source: visit the Vatican online. Find information on the Holy Father,

the Roman Curia, and Vatican News Services; visit the Vatican museums and find information on Jubilee 2000. You can also search the Vatican archives for documents dealing with issues such as catechism and documents of the second Vatican Council.

The Catholic Pages
(http://www.catholic-pages.com/)
"This site is filled with information about the Catholic Church and the Catholic religion. You'll find information on the Pope and the Cardinals, the Virgin Mary and angels, Vatican City and the dioceses of the world, saints and sin, the mass and marriage . . . even some Catholic jokes!"

The Catholic Mother's Internet Connection
(http://www.qni.com/~catholic/mom.htm)
This website is specially designed for Roman Catholic mothers. "It's tough raising children in our world today. The challenge of bringing our kids up in the wonderfully rich traditions of the Roman Catholic faith are numerous. It is my hope that this site will serve as a resource center for us, and will be updated with the latest information and news relevant to being a Catholic mother today."

Jewish

Aleph
(http://www.aleph.org/)
This is a Jewish Renewal website dealing with theological issues from that perspective.

Jewish University In CyberspacE (J.U.I.C.E.)
(http://www.wzo.org.il/juice/index.htm)
This "cyber-university" offers free courses on a variety of topics of Jewish interest. Course lectures are sent via e-mail, to be read and studied at your convenience. There is also an opportunity for discussion with the instructor and other course participants.

SpiritQuest
(http://www.wizard.net/~kc/lsc/spiritquest.htm)
"SpiritQuest is a site for Jews, prospective Jews, and non-Jews seeking deeper spiritual fulfillment, ways to incorporate meaningful Jewish ritual into their lives, and/or general information about Judaism. It is written primarily from a Reform Jewish perspective, but issues are explored from all points of view."

Torah on the Information Superhighway
(http://www.torah.org/)
This is one of many sites devoted to the study of the Torah and associated topics. It also offers "a wide (and growing) range of classes to Jewish seekers across the Internet, on Jewish philosophy, liturgy, ethics, and law."

The Mining Company Judaism Site
(http://judaism.miningco.com/)
This is an eclectic site containing information on and links to a wide variety of Jewish topics, including Sabbath candle-lighting traditions and times, to Hebrew software, Kabbalah, Jewish websites for children, recipes, and the weekly Torah portion.

Islam

Islamic Information and News Network
(http://www.islamfaq.com/)
This website contains general information on Islam, as well as a list of frequently asked questions (FAQs) about it. It also includes a discussion of Islamic issues, news, images of holy places, and important religious dates.

al-Muslim
(http://www.al-muslim.org/)
This website contains an introduction to Islam, as well as information on the Holy Qur'an, science in the Qur'an, women in Islam, and articles on a variety of Islamic topics.

The Holy Qur'an Online
(http://dana.ucc.nau.edu/~ksaa/saad/islam2.html)
This website focuses on the Holy Qur'an, offering it in Arabic and in various translations. There is an index of the Qur'an by topic, chapter, and word, as well as a list of articles covering a wide variety of topics.

Muslim World Yellow Pages
(http://www.muslim-yellowpages.com/)
This site facilitates easy access to nonreligious sites of interest to Muslims. It lists, for example, embassies in the United States and around the world that are of interest to Muslims, news, career and travel information, a business directory, a list of mosques around the world, as well as a Muslim marriage matchmaking service.

Protestant

The Mining Company Christianity—Protestantism Site
(http://protestantism.miningco.com/)
A general site containing links to such topics as church history, devotional tools, integrating faith and life, sacraments and locations of Protestant churches categorized by denomination. It also contains links to, for example, Assemblies of God, Mennonite Church, Moravian Church, Presbyterian Church, Religious Society of Friends, United Church of Christ, etc.

Mormon

The Official Web Site of the Church of Jesus Christ of Latter-day Saints
(http://www.lds.org/)
This site covers the basic beliefs of the religion as well as information on the Mormon family history resources, member resources, and media information.

All about Mormons
(http://www.mormons.org/)
This wide-ranging website is designed "to explain the beliefs and practices of

the Church of Jesus Christ of Latter-day Saints." It contains frequently asked questions (FAQs), a variety of articles dealing with basic religious beliefs, LDS news and a link to LDS Radio, a glossary of LDS terms, and even a section on LDS humor.

Unitarian/Universalist

Unitarian Universalist Association
(`http://uua.org/main.html`)
This site provides outlines of traditions and beliefs, with news, articles, and indexes of Unitarian Universalist people and places, both congregations and websites.

Unitarian Universalist Buddhist Fellowship
(`http://www.uua.org/uubf/`)
This website explores the beliefs and practices common to Buddhists and Unitarian Universalists. It contains a FAQ listing, and information on where UUBF study groups are located around the United States.

Buddhist

The Cultivation Page
(`http://members.xoom.com/cultivation/`)
A nonreligious approach to Buddhism, introducing the "Eight Consciousness" theory of the Buddha and introducing daily wisdom through the "Hundred Parables of Zen."

DharmaNet International
(`http://www.dharmanet.org/`)
A site that considers itself "A Gateway to Buddhism," it offers links to Buddhist study resources, art, essays, locations and schedules for meditation retreats, etc.

Hindu

Hindu Resources Online
(http://www.hindu.org/)
A source for information on Hindu organizations, leaders, and resources. It contains articles on religion as well as news and lists of upcoming events.

Hinduism Today
(http://www.hinduismtoday.kauai.hi.us/ashram/htoday.html)
A website developed to "foster Hindu solidarity as a 'unity in diversity' among all sects and lineages; to inform and inspire Hindus worldwide and people interested in Hinduism; to dispel myths, illusions, and misinformation about Hinduism; to protect, preserve, and promote the sacred Vedas and the Hindu religion, especially the Nandinatha Sampradaya; to nurture a truly spiritual Hindu renaissance."

Genealogy

Are you interested in finding out more about your ancestors? The Internet provides you with powerful tools that were unavailable just a decade ago.

The Genealogy Home Page
(http://www.genhomepage.com/)
A website containing a wide variety of links to genealogical resources on the Internet. Links are categorized by such topics as "Religious Genealogy Resources," "Internet Genealogy Guides," "Genealogy Societies," and "Upcoming Genealogy Events."

World-Wide Genealogy Resources
(http://www.genhomepage.com/world.html)
This site contains hundreds of links to genealogy websites around the world, ranging from African American, Australian, Basque, and Belgian to Switzer-

land, the U.K., and the United States. If you are serious about beginning or continuing a quest for your ancestors who came from another country, this is a wonderful site to visit.

GenForum
(http://genforum.familytreemaker.com/general/)
This site contains a group of targeted message boards on which users can post their questions. The message boards are broken down by state and by country, as well as by topic area, such as adoption ("seeking birthson born 4/18/74 in Memphis"), Jews ("seeking people from Faleshty"), obituaries, Quakers ("Quakers in Barbados 1640-1800"), and the American Revolution ("218th anniversary of Battle at the Cowpens").

Online Genealogical Database Index
(http://www.gentree.com/)
This extensive Genealogical Database Index claims to have links "to all known genealogical databases searchable through the Web." If you are looking for information for the Ackley family down to the Zix or Zwojda family, this would be a good site to check to see if anyone else has already begun the search.

Government

Information from the United States government can be a mouse click away. Notice that governmental website URLs end with ".gov", rather than ".com".

The White House
(http://www.whitehouse.gov/)
Visit the home of the president of the United States; learn about the president, the vice president, and their families; take a tour of the White House; and link to commonly requested federal services.

The Department of State
(http://www.state.gov/)
Read the latest U.S. State Department international policies or download the

forms to apply for a passport. Consular information sheets are available for every country of the world. They include such information as location of the U.S. embassy or consulate in the subject country, unusual immigration practices, health conditions, minor political disturbances, unusual currency and entry regulations, crime and security information, and drug penalties. Also, travel warnings are issued when the state department decides, based on all relevant information, to recommend that Americans avoid travel to a certain country.

Postal Service ZIP Code Lookup
(`http://www.usps.gov/ncsc/`)
Need a ZIP code for a snail-mail address? Here's where to find it.

The Library of Congress
(`http://lcweb.loc.gov/`)
Search the Library of Congress catalogs and collections without traveling to Washington. Visit the fascinating American Memory collection, which offers multimedia collections of digitized documents, photographs, recorded sound, moving pictures, and text from the Library's Americana collections.

You might also want to visit the library page devoted to Internet guides, tutorials, and training information

(`http://lcweb.loc.gov/global/internet/training.html`)

that are provided by organizations outside the Library.

The Federal Web Locator
(`http://www.law.vill.edu/fed-agency/fedwebloc.html`)
This is *the* place to come if you need to locate a website for any U.S. government agency, a governmental consortium or quasi-governmental agency (e.g., National Academy of Sciences, Smithsonian Institution), a federal commission (e.g., Postal Rate Commission), or any of a number of organizations not directly connected to the U.S. government (e.g., United Nations, World Bank, CSPAN). This website is provided by the Center for Information Law and Policy, a joint initiative of the Villanova University School of Law and the

Illinois Institute of Technology's Chicago-Kent College of Law. It is "intended to be the one-stop shopping point for federal government information on the World Wide Web."

National Aeronautics and Space Administration (NASA)
(http://www.nasa.gov/)
Interested in the latest on space flight? Here's where to find the latest NASA information, as well as where to follow space shuttle flights moment by moment. You will also find photo, video, and audio galleries recording the history of NASA projects.

Cooking/Recipes

Epicurious Food
(http://food.epicurious.com/)
Listed as the site "for people who eat," Epicurious Food is an umbrella website encompassing *Gourmet Magazine, Bon Appétit,* a database of over 8,000 recipes, a dictionary of culinary terms, and more. Do you need to know how to mix a Brave Bull (2 ounces tequila, 1 ounce Kahlua) for a friend? The recipe is here. Are you stuck in your kitchen with excess truffle oil and no recipe for it comes to mind? Here are recipes for pizza with truffle oil, truffled lobster risotto (why didn't you think of that?!), and penne di bosco.

Culinary.com
(http://www.culinary.com/)
There are over 73,000 recipes in the culinary.com searchable database, including breakfast items, Cajun dishes, ethnic recipes, and even more than 250 recipes for Spam. Also, follow the late-breaking news from the world of food. Which famous chef has moved to which new restaurant? What is the latest news on Twinkies? Links allow you to subscribe to such food-related mailing lists as "Pasta Lovers Newsletter" or the Danish mailing list on food and nutrition, with all discussion conducted in Danish. Indeed, an eclectic culinary site.

The Global Gastronomer
(`http://www.cs.yale.edu/homes/hupfer/global/`
`gastronomer.html`)
This website is devoted to cuisines of the world. Click on a geographic region on the world map and browse a wide array of articles and recipes from that region, categorized by country. It also contains a number of links to other ethnic food websites, as well as major recipe archives.

Culinary Café
(`http://www.culinarycafe.com/`)
Recipes, hints, tips, and suggestions for kitchen appliances and gadgets you never realized you can't live without. You'll find food news here, as well as links to other food-related websites. Finally, if you can't locate the recipe you are seeking, post a question on their bulletin board for others to see and respond to.

The Searchable Online Archive of Recipes (SOAR)
(`http://SOAR.Berkeley.edu/recipes/`)
This site claims to contain over 40,000 recipes that you can search by keyword. Browse through such categories as "soups & stuff," "on the side," "holiday foods," and "restricted and special diets." It also has recipes categorized by geographic area and encompassing a variety of ethnicities within that area (e.g., for North/South America, it includes Argentinian, Brazilian, Cajun, Canadian, Caribbean, Colombian, Eskimo, Mexican, Native American, Peruvian, and Venezuelan).

TuDocs
(`http://www.tudocs.com/`)
Billing itself as "The Ultimate Directory of Cooking Sites," this website contains links to other cooking websites and lists them by category. For example, you can find sites related to breakfast, canning, diabetic recipes, outdoor cooking, vegetarian cuisines, and more.

Hobbies

Perhaps you find yourself with somewhat more leisure time on your hands. It's a great opportunity to see what information you can find on your favorite old or new hobby.

Quilting

World Wide Quilting Page
(`http://www.quilt.com/MainQuiltingPage.html`)
This page includes information on both basic and advanced quilting techniques, designs and directions for blocks of various sizes, a block of the month, and "lots of fun and surprises for individuals or groups" in the form of mystery quilts. You will also find links to other quilting sites on the Internet.

Collecting

If you or someone you know collects anything, chances are good that other people somewhere do, too. Connect with other collectors online!

Pen Collectors of America
(`http://www.pencentral.com/`)
"Pen Collectors of America (PCA) is a nonprofit association dedicated to providing information and assistance to all pen collectors, expanding the interest in collecting beautiful vintage pens, helping new pen collectors get started, providing a forum for collectors' issues, and supporting local pen groups nationwide."

Matchbox International Collectors Association
(`http://www.matchboxclub.com/`)
This international organization is devoted to support of collectors of Matchbox toys.

The Rushlight Club: Collectors of Early Lighting
(http://www.rushlight.org/)
This website is for collectors of antique lighting devices. Its purpose is to "stimulate an interest in the study of early lighting, including the use of lighting devices and lighting fuels and the origins and development of each by means of written articles, lectures, conferences, exhibitions from private collections, and, if desired, through the medium of exchange, and its object shall be to collect, preserve, and disseminate information and data obtained through these studies."

Still Bank Collectors Club of America
(http://www.stillbankclub.com/)
"The objectives of the organization shall be to stimulate the knowledge of, interest in, and the collection of antique and contemporary still banks, and further, within the limits of friendly rivalry, to assist members in adding to and enhancing the value of their collections of such banks."

North American Society of Pipe Collectors
(http://www.naspc.org/)
"The North American Society of Pipe Collectors was founded after a long evening spent over a pot of good coffee and more than a bowl or two of good tobacco. Phil Bradford and Regis McCafferty decided that a club was needed in Ohio to promote pipe smoking, information sharing, knowledge of tobaccos, and fellowship with other pipe smokers."

Lionel Collectors Club of America
(http://www.lionelcollectors.org/)
"The LCCA was founded by James D. Gates of Des Moines, Iowa, on August 1, 1970. It was his idea that collectors and operators of Lionel trains had long needed an organization dedicated solely to their hobby interest. With this basis, Jim placed ads in the railroading magazines inviting others of similar interests to join Jim in establishing a club. By July 1, 1971, eighty-three charter members had signed on to give birth to his new club exclusively for the Lionel hobbyist.

Since then our membership has continued to increase to where today there over ten thousand members of the LCCA worldwide."

The Whittle Mark
(http://home.att.net/~fred-taylor/)
"Our mandate is to promote a social environment for collectors to meet, discuss, and research the history of America through the collecting as well as buying, trading, and selling of antique bottles and glass."

The U.K. Sucrologists Club
(http://web.ukonline.co.uk/email.ukscsugar/)
This international club is for collectors of "the little packets of sugar you get when you order tea or coffee in a cafe or a restaurant. There are thousands of different ones—square, rectangular, tube-shaped, some plain and simple, right up to the really exotic multicoloured ones."

The Statue of Liberty Collectors' Club
(http://www.statueoflibertyclub.com/meet.html)
This website is for people who collect memorabilia associated with the Statue of Liberty.

Antique Automobile Club of America
(http://www.aaca.org/)
The Antique Automobile Club of America is the world's oldest and largest automotive historical society. It is dedicated to the preservation, restoration, and maintenance of automobiles and automotive history.

Gardening

Garden Web
(http://www.gardenweb.com/)
The Garden Web forums may constitute the largest community of gardeners on

the Internet. In the forums you can find out information from professionals and lay experts on a wide variety of plants and growing regions and on plant care and landscaping issues. You can search their databases for information on plant societies and clubs, as well as botanical and common names for plants.

National Gardening Association
(`http://www.garden.org/`)
The National Gardening Association is designed to help gardeners. You can search the database of articles that have appeared in *National Gardening* magazine and browse or search through questions that have been asked by others and answered by a professional horticulturist. You can also sign up for an on-line educational course (e.g., "Exploring the World of Plants: A Botany Course for Gardeners"), use the 15,000-entry horticulture dictionary, or find links to suppliers of rare seeds and plants.

The North American Rock Garden Society (NARGS)
(`http://www.garden.org/links/links.html`)
NARGS "is for gardening enthusiasts interested in alpine, saxatile, and low-growing perennials. It encourages the study and cultivation of wildflowers that grow well among rocks, whether such plants originate above treeline or at lower elevations. Through its publications, meetings, and garden visits, NARGS provides extensive opportunities for both beginners and experts to expand their knowledge of plant cultivation and propagation and of construction, maintenance, and design of special interest gardens. Woodland gardens, bog gardens, raised beds, planted walls, container gardens, and alpine berms are all addressed."

Golf

GolfWeb
(`http://www.golfweb.com/gwab.htm`)
Billing itself as the site for "Everything Golf on the World Wide Web," GolfWeb not only gives you links to golf websites in Japan and Europe, but also has five sections entitled "Your Game." Here are articles and tips on the proper selection of equipment, rules of golf and etiquette, game improvement, and more. Packing your clubs on your next trip? This site contains a searchable golf course guide listing over 21,000 public and private courses in the U.S., Canada, Australia, Japan, and throughout Europe. Of course, there is a pro shop for purchasing merchandise, as well as discussion groups covering various aspects of the game. GolfWeb is the PGA European Tour's Official Internet/Web Partner, providing extensive coverage of all European Tour events.

Golf Online.com
(`http://www.golfonline.com/`)
This site is produced by the editors of *Golf* magazine and is updated daily. Besides news from the PGA, LPGA, Seniors, European, Nike tours, and the USGA, this site also provides hints to improve your game, information on equipment, courses, and special information on women's golf.

Virtual Golfer
(`http://www.golfball.com/`)
Billing itself as "Your Complete Internet Golfing Resource," this site provides access to *Greenside* online magazine; the pro shop, providing equipment, collectibles, and accessories; a directory of courses and accommodations; online tips ranging from fundamentals to advanced shotmaking; and information on PGA, LPGA, and Senior PGA tour schedules.

Fishing

Federation of Fly Fishers
(http://www.fedflyfishers.org/index2.shtml)
Their motto is, "Conserving, Restoring, Educating . . . Through Fly Fishing."

Reel-Time
(http://www.reel-time.com/)
The Internet journal of saltwater fly fishing.

World Wide Angler
(http://www.chesapeakeangler.com/)
An online fishing magazine with articles, news, links, and message boards.

The Norwegian Flyshop
(http://www.flyshop.no/)
The one-stop shopping guide to sportfishing in Norway.

FISHTHEWEB.COM
(http://www.fishtheweb.com/)
"Taking fishing into the twenty-first century. Fishing reports, fishing articles, photos, weather, tides, fish feeding times, maps, guides, fishing clubs, marinas, boats, fishing tackle, fishing accessories, and more."

Skiing

Great Outdoor Recreation Pages
(http://www.gorp.com/gorp/activity/skiing.htm)
"GORP's Skiing and Snowsports Page offers a lively array of feature articles on cross-country skiing, downhill skiing, and snowboarding, combined with a thorough regional ski guide, round-ups of the top resorts, forums, articles and links for snowmobilers, a directory of ski trips, and much more."

SKIING Magazine, the Magazine of Winter Adventure
(http://www.skinet.com/newsstand/skiing/)
"Captures the excitement and thrill of skiing and provides practical information to help you squeeze maximum pleasure from your time in the mountains."

Hyperski
(http://www.hyperski.com/index.htm)
An online magazine for skiing and snowboarding, with information on ski lessons, conditions, travel/tours, heli-skiing, equipment, ski resorts, and snowboarding.

Cross Country Ski Areas Association
(http://www.xcski.org/)
This website contains information on cross country and Nordic ski areas, racing, equipment, cross-country ski publications, snow conditions, snowshoeing, cross-country skiing facts and terminology, as well as links to other cross-country websites.

Walking

Hiking and Walking Home Page
(http://www.teleport.com/~walking/hiking.html)
A site with links to places to go hiking throughout the world, tours, a calendar of walking events, and chat rooms devoted to walking, backpacking, exercise, and camping.

The Mining Co. Guide to Walking
(http://walking.miningco.com/?pid=2756&cob=home)
This site contains articles covering a variety of facets of walking, ranging from information on how your muscles moved you from here to there to the health benefits of walking, walking techniques, injury prevention, and pedestrian activism. You will find all these and many more topics at this fascinating and diverse site.

Reading

The Book Group List

(`http://books.rpmdp.com/`)

"Have you ever entered a library, inhaling the musty perfume of thousands of books and felt euphoric? When you go to a bookstore, do the books seem to leap from the shelves into your hands? Do you have precarious piles of books covering all available surfaces in your home just waiting to be read? Does your spouse ever warn you that your house is about to collapse under the weight of books?" If so, this is the place for you. Book reviews, recommendations, and more.

BookBrowser: The Guide for Avid Readers

(`http://www.bookbrowser.com/`)

This site offers reading lists, book reviews, titles of forthcoming books, as well as information on a wide variety of authors.

Games

Bridge—a fascinating card game!

(`http://web.math.auc.dk/~nwp/bridge/`)

This site offers a wide variety of links to sites including national and international bridge organizations, tournaments around the world, bridge education and training, newsgroups and mailing lists devoted to the game, bridge magazines, and even Internet sites where you can play bridge against other players who are online at the time.

The Internet Bridge Archive

(`http://rgb.anu.edu.au/Bridge/`)

This website modestly claims to contain "anything and everything electronically available that is related to the card game (nay, sport!) of bridge." Here you will find links to a wide variety of bridge clubs and organizations, information on bridge and computers, tournaments, tips on how to play, and references to books and bridge newsgroups.

World Bridge Federation
(http://www.bridge.gr/wbf.htm)
Find out what's happening in bridge competitions around the world. Locate links to bridge players' organizations throughout the world and find tips for improving your game.

American Cribbage Congress
(http://www.cribbage.org/)
Since 1980 the ACC has generated interest in cribbage by promoting the growth of local clubs, sanctioning tournaments, standardizing the rules of play, and creating programs to teach the young.

U.S. Chess Online
(http://www.uschess.org/)
The U.S. Chess Federation is the official sanctioning body for tournament chess in the United States and for U.S. participation in international chess events. Drop by here for news stories and press releases on this game, information on tournaments, and tips on improving your game.

Movies

Are you wondering what movie to see this evening and interested in looking over a review or two before you decide? Investigate this gateway to a broad collection of sites.

Movie Review Query Database
(http://www.mrqe.com/lookup?)
This database claims links to over 90,000 reviews of more than 15,000 movies. Type in the name of the movie you are interested in, and this website will list links to as many different reviewers as it can find. Reviewers range from the general mainstream, like *Time* magazine and the *New York Times*, to the offbeat, like the Flick Filosopher, the Film Geek, and the Cranky Critic, to special interest reviews, like *Christian Spotlight on the Movies* and *Screen It! Entertainment*

Reviews for Parents. For a sense of the coverage of movies at this website, *Casablanca* (1942) has links to 29 reviews, and *Titanic* (1997) has links to 209.

Pets

American Veterinary Medical Association
(http://www.avma.org/)
This is a site for animal lovers to visit to find out about pet care and animal health. If you are interested in taking up a new profession at this point in life, there is also information on careers in veterinary medicine.

The Pet Channel
(http://www.thepetchannel.com/)
This is a great place for information on finding a pet, keeping it healthy, locating it if it is lost, dealing with separation anxiety (your pet's—not yours), introducing new pets into your household, or even finding your pet's horoscope.

The National Committee on Pot Bellied Pigs
(http://www.ncopp.com/)
Come here to find out everything you ever wanted to know about this wonderful pet.

The Oregon Ferret Association
(http://oregon-ferret.org/)
All you ever wanted to know about ferrets as pets and a source for ferret mugs and T-shirts. You can find out about the OFA's Ferret Fun Match, the premier ferret event of the Pacific Northwest. Join other ferret owners, veterinarians, and vendors for ferret games, informative talks, health checks, fund-raising promotions, and lots of fun!

National Alternative Pet Association
(http://www.altpet.net/index.html)
"Is your pet *unconventional?* Do people put you down because your pet isn't a

socially acceptable cat, dog, or goldfish? Do you prefer the companionship of a domestic ferret, sugar glider, hedgehog, gerbil, snake, lizard, prairie dog, domestic skunk, degu, wallaby, emu, parrot, millipede, llama, exotic cat, monkey or . . . ? Do you have trouble finding information on how to properly keep your alternative pets? Is it hard to find veterinarians, shelters, rescue groups, or even food and supplies for your exotic pets?" This is the site for you!

The Happy Hermit: How to Keep Your Hermit Crab Happy!
(`http://www.geocities.com/Heartland/Hills/9459/`)
A website for fledgling or experienced hermit crab owners. Topics covered include why to buy a hermit crab, advice on purchasing your hermit, where to buy and what to look for, how to tell a hermit crab's age, hermit housing and lighting, caring for your hermit crab, temperature, moisture, food, treats, handling, and exercise. What more could one want to know about hermit crabs?

Hermit World
(`http://208.240.134.42/hermitworld/`)
If you can't find the hermit crab information you're looking for at the previous site, here's another place to try.

American Tarantula Society
(`http://torgo.cnchost.com/ats/`)
The largest arachnid society in the world, devoted to the care, feeding, and promotion of tarantulas, other spiders, scorpions, and other arachnid orders as pets.

The Pede Page
(`http://www.ilinkusa.net/~100legs/`)
Did you know that centipedes and millipedes are growing in popularity as terrarium pets? You would, if you visited this site. Some of the larger centipedes make spectacular display animals.

Volunteerism

Peace Corps
(http://www.peacecorps.gov/)
Remember how you thought about going into the Peace Corps back in the 60s? It's not too late. There is no upper age limit to serving as a Peace Corps volunteer. The Peace Corps website says that "the countries where Volunteers serve often welcome and value the wealth of experience that older Americans bring to their overseas assignments."

America's Promise—The Alliance for Youth
(http://www.americaspromise.org/)
Chaired by General Colin L. Powell, USA (Ret), America's Promise is "a national crusade to improve the lives of our nation's youth. Established at the Presidents' Summit for America's Future in Philadelphia in April of 1997 and endorsed by every living U.S. President, America's Promise aims to ensure all children in America have access to the fundamental resources needed to build and strengthen them to become responsible, productive adults."

VolunteerMatch
(http://www.volunteermatch.org/)
VolunteerMatch has partnered with thousands of nonprofit organizations throughout the United States to build a database of volunteer opportunities that you can search by ZIP code. When I entered my ZIP code into the search form and indicated that I could volunteer on a fairly regular basis (in contrast to one time only) and that I would be willing to volunteer only within five miles of my home, VolunteerMatch came up with thirty opportunities for me, in organizations including a foster home program, the local public radio station, a journal on international wildlife law, and a cancer center.

Folks Our Age

AARP Webplace
(http://www.aarp.org/)
Visit the homepage of the American Association of Retired Persons. From here you can access information on becoming a member of the association as well as find a large number of links to topics ranging from legislative issues to leisure and fun.

ThirdAge
(http://www.thirdage.com/cgi-bin/rd/nltw/)
"ThirdAge (thurd'aj): (n.) 1. A time of life characterized by happiness, freedom, and learning. 2. A life stage following 'youth' and preceding 'old age'. 3. A Website where like-minded people find intelligent conversations and useful tools. 4. Your best years yet! ThirdAge.com is the online home of a vibrant on-line society filled with ideas and interactions generated, hosted, and reflected by the views of its citizens—the ThirdAgers themselves."

Boomers International
(http://members.aol.com/boomersint/boomone.html)
A website by and for members of the baby boom generation. Besides bulletin boards and shopping links, there are also hyperlinks to boomer timelines, a "where are they now" section, "cultures, countercultures, and subcultures," hobbies, news articles, and "oldies but goodies" musical links.

The Senior Center
(http://www.senior-center.com/)
"If you're over fifty . . . or have a friend or loved one who is . . . then you're definitely at the right place. Come on in and pull up a chair."

You'll find information here on health, wealth, home, hobbies, sex life, gardening, genealogy, jokes, and vacations. There are also links to assist you in sending an e-mail message to the president of the United States, your senator, or your representative in Congress.

You will also find more whimsical information here, like "Do You Remember When?" or "Stories and Recipes of the Great Depression."

An eclectic, enjoyable site.

The Interactive Aging Network
(http://www.ianet.org/)
"The Interactive Aging Network is a not-for-profit corporation dedicated to serving organizations that provide services to older adults."

There is information here on resources for seniors on such topics as health, news, sports, travel, career development, health-care providers, housing options, etc. It is a site rich in information and worthy of a visit.

Administration on Aging
(http://www.aoa.dhhs.gov/)
The Administration on Aging is a division of the U.S. Department of Health and Human Services. This website provides you with information regarding the Administration on Aging and its programs. It also has links to numerous aging-related websites that deal with a wide variety of topics.

Elderhostel
(http://www.elderhostel.org/)
"Elderhostel is a nonprofit organization providing educational adventures all over the world to adults aged 55 and over. Study the literature of Jane Austen in the White Mountains of New Hampshire, or travel to Greece to explore the spectacular art and architecture of its ancient civilization, or conduct field research in Belize to save the endangered dolphin population. Elderhostel is for people on the move who believe learning is a lifelong process."

Transitions
Retirement

The Retirement Net
(http://www.retirenet.com/)
This is a website containing hyperlinks to retirement communities; independent living, assisted living, and nursing care facilities; and resorts and rentals available in retirement communities.

The Nolo.com Self Help Law Center
(http://www.nolo.com/ChunkOA/OA.index.html)
This website contains information and links on social security, pensions, general retirement information, Medicare and Medicaid, and long-term health care.

Divorce

Divorcesource.com
(http://www.divorcesource.com/)
Divorcesource.com is a comprehensive informational network for divorce support. They have not only bulletin board forums and live chat rooms, but also links to family law services, articles on divorce, and links for all fifty states and Canadian provinces to divorce attorneys, statistics, legal requirements for divorce, information on child custody, spousal support, taxes, etc.

Divorcenet
(http://www.divorcenet.com/)
This website has a wide variety of information to assist individuals going through divorce. Content ranges from a state-by-state review of legal issues to information on divorce mediation, domestic violence, grandparents' issues, military divorce, and stepfamily concerns. There are also divorce FAQs and links to other divorce-related websites.

Hospice Care/Death

Hospice Foundation of America
(http://www.hospicefoundation.org/)
This website provides basic education regarding hospice care, how to select a hospice, and how to locate one near you. You can also read first-person accounts of loved ones dying in a hospice environment.

Hospice Web
(http://www.teleport.com/~hospice/)
"Hospice care is a choice you make to enhance life for a dying person. A person with a terminal disease may choose to die at home with the support of family, friends, and caring professionals. Hospice care emphasizes comfort measures and counseling to provide social, spiritual, and physical support to the dying patient and his or her family. All hospice care is under professional medical supervision."

Death and Dying
(http://www.death-dying.com/)
The old cliché tells us that death is one of the inevitables in this world. Yet many of us have very little experience in either watching a loved one die or supporting people who are in that position. This website can be a valuable starting point when you are learning about this area of human experience.

There are first-person articles here as well as information on terminal illnesses, loss of a spouse, sudden or tragic deaths, dos and don'ts for supporting those who are grieving, and links to a number of other related websites.

WidowNet
(http://www.fortnet.org/WidowNet/)
WidowNet is an "information and self-help resource for, and by, widows and widowers. Topics covered include grief, bereavement, recovery, and other information helpful to people of all ages, religious backgrounds, and sexual orientations who have suffered the death of a spouse or life partner."

People Finders

The purpose of these sites is discussed in Chapter 4. They are listed here for your convenience.

WhoWhere!
(www.whowhere.com)

Four11—The Internet White Pages
(http://www.four11.com/)

InfoSpace
(http://www.infospace.com/)

Switchboard
(http://netfind.switchboard.com/)

AOL NetFind
(http://www.aol.com/netfind/emailfinder.adp)

Yahoo! People Search
(http://people.yahoo.com/)

Netscape People Finder
(http://home.netscape.com/netcenter/whitepages.html)

Search Engines

Search engines are discussed in detail in Chapter 5. They are listed here for your convenience.

Alta Vista
(http://altavista.com)

HotBot
(http://www.hotbot.com)

Ask Jeeves
(http://www.askjeeves.com/)

Excite
(http://www.excite.com/)

Infoseek
(http://infoseek.go.com/)

Northern Light
(http://www.northernlight.com/)

Lycos
(http://www.lycos.com/)

Yahoo!
(http://www.yahoo.com/)

Meta-search Engines

Meta-search engines conduct searches of several search engines. They are cussed in greater detail in Chapter 5. Some of the best-known meta-sea engines are listed below.

Metacrawler
(`http://www.go2net.com/search.html`)

Dogpile
(`http://www.dogpile.com/`)

Inference Find
(`http://www.infind.com/`)

Mailing List Locators

L-Soft international
(`http://www.lsoft.com/lists/listref.html`)
This is the definitive site to visit to locate LISTSERVE-based mailing lists.

Publicly Accessible Mailing Lists
(`http://www.neosoft.com/internet/paml`)
This site posts newly discovered public mailing lists about every month. It egorizes mailing lists alphabetically by topic area. If, for example, you are lo ing for a mailing list dealing with the Cherokee language, you will find Tsalagi List for all students of the Tsalagi (Cherokee) language. (There twenty-seven list members currently.) If quilting is your passion, join Quil (`info@quiltart.com`).

Newsgroup Locators

Liszt's Usenet Newsgroups Directory
(`http://liszt.bluemarble.net/news`)
A powerful, easy-to-use website that allows you search for newsgroups of interest to you.

CyberPulse
(`http://www.webcom.com/impulse/`)
"All you ever wanted to know about e-mail discussion groups (mailing lists), including . . . an introduction to mailing list manager commands where you will learn how to subscribe and unsubscribe to discussion groups; links to other websites where you can search for discussion groups on any subject."

Reference.com
(`http://www.reference.com/`)
Another site you can use to locate mailing lists and newsgroups of interest to you.

Internet Chat Programs

AOL Instant Messenger (AIM)
(`http://aol.com`)

ICQ (pronounced "I seek you")
(`http://www.icq.com`)

Microsoft Chat
(`http://www.windowsupdate.com`)

MIRC
(`http://www.mirc.com`)

Computer AntiVirus Programs

McAfee VirusScan
(`http://www.mcafee.com/`)

Norton AntiVirus
(`http://www.symantec.com/nav/`)

Dr Solomon's AntiVirus
(`http://antivirus.drsolomon.com/`)

Computer Virus Hoax Information

Symantec AntiVirus Research Center Hoax Information
(`http://www.symantec.com/avcenter/hoax.html`)

Computer Incident Advisory Capability (CAIC), a
division of the United States Department of Energy
(`http://ciac.llnl.gov/ciac/CIACHoaxes.html`)

Computer Virus Myths
(`http://www.kumite.com/myths/home.htm`)

Computing Ease

Logitech
(`http://www.logitech.com`)
A manufacturer of, among other things, wonderful mice, trackballs, and other
input devices that are ergonomically designed to make your computing life
more comfortable and productive.

Dragon
(`http://www.dragonsys.com`)
The manufacturer of NaturallySpeaking, a powerful and accurate speech recognition software product. Why type your e-mails when you can dictate them and let your computer type them for you? NaturallySpeaking is an alternative to much of your typing, but its accuracy depends upon your taking the time to train it to the way you speak. The more you train it, the more accurate it will become.

ViaVoice
(`http://www.software.ibm.com/speech/`)
A powerful competitive product to Dragon NaturallySpeaking. It, too, will perform admirably, provided you train it to recognize your speech patterns and continue training it as you use it. Like NaturallySpeaking, ViaVoice increases its skill at recognizing your words.

Just for Fun

Spam Haiku
(`http://pemtropics.mit.edu/~jcho/spam/`)
This is one of the very first totally, amazingly, and utterly useless websites I discovered on the Internet. It is still one of my favorites, in large part because it is so unlikely. This site contains over 12,000 haiku poems, all related to the tinned meat product, Spam. For example:

> SPAM is big in Greece.
> With filo dough, feta, for
> Spamakopita.

(Reprinted here with the permission of the author and webmaster of the Spam Haiku website, John Y. N. Cho.)

The Web's First Shaggy Dog Story Archive
(`http://www.awpi.com/Combs/Shaggy/index.html`)
If you are a punster, drop by to read hundreds of brief stories that all end with

terrible puns. For example, in a story entitled "Nostalgia for the 60s," the contrived two-paragraph story leads to the punch line "Peas would rule the planets, and love would clear the bars. It was the dawning of the age of asparagus."

The Centre for the Easily Amused
(`http://www.amused.com/`)
No more and no less than it claims. Daily jokes, a list of life's little annoyances and thoughts you wouldn't want to live by, as well as links to sites such as "Short Attention-Span Site of the Week" or "Sites of Dubious Taste."

Free Stuff to Clutter Your House With
(`http://www.crecon.com/home/free.html`)
If you just live for the free product samples that come with your daily newspaper or in the mail, this is the website for you. Come here to receive samples of products, free issues of magazines, and much more that you probably don't need.

The Useless Pages
(`http://www.go2net.com/internet/useless/`)
Do you have time to kill? This page contains links to an amazing number of totally useless pages. Drop by to witness for yourself how much effort goes into creating absolutely trivial, silly, and useless websites.

Trendy Magic
(`http://trendy.org/magic/interactivemagic.html`)
Magic on the Internet! Go try it. You will be amazed!

UselessKnowledge.com
(`http://www.uselessknowledge.com/`)
Laying claim to being the most useful site on the Internet for useless knowledge, this site offers trivia, quotes, quizzes, useless facts, and much more. You can even come by and find out how many days remain until Y3K—the year 3000.

Appendix A

International Abbreviations

For those of you who wonder just how far and wide the Internet stretches, different countries of origin have different abbreviations near or at the end of their URLs. For example, the URL of the Vatican website is `http://www.vatican.va/`, ending with the two letter country abbreviation, "VA," while the URL for the Mongolia Online is `http://www.magic.mn/`, ending in "MN," the abbreviation for Mongolia.

Country	Abbreviation	Country	Abbreviation
Afghanistan	AF	Barbados	BB
Albania	AL	Belarus	BY
Algeria	DZ	Belgium	BE
American Samoa	AS	Belize	BZ
Andorra	AD	Benin	BJ
Angola	AO	Bermuda	BM
Anguilla	AI	Bhutan	BT
Antarctica	AQ	Bolivia	BO
Antigua and Barbuda	AG	Bosnia and Herzegovina	BA
Argentina	AR	Botswana	BW
Armenia	AM	Bouvet Island	BV
Aruba	AW	Brazil	BR
Australia	AU	Brunei Darussalam	BN
Austria	AT	Bulgaria	BG
Azerbaijan	AZ	Burkina Faso	BF
Bahamas	BS	Burundi	BI
Bahrain	BH	Cambodia	KH
Bangladesh	BD	Cameroon	CM

Country	Abbreviation	Country	Abbreviation
Cape Verde	CV	France	FR
Cayman Islands	KY	France, Metropolitan	FX
Central African Republic	CF	French Guiana	GF
Chad	TD	French Polynesia	PF
Chile	CL	French Southern Territories	TF
China	CN	Gabon	GA
Christmas Island	CX	Gambia	GM
Colombia	CO	Georgia	GE
Comoros	KM	Germany	DE
Congo	CG	Ghana	GH
Cook Islands	CK	Gibraltar	GI
Costa Rica	CR	Greece	GR
Cote D'Ivoire (Ivory Coast)	CI	Greenland	GL
Croatia	HR	Grenada	GD
Cuba	CU	Guadeloupe	GP
Cyprus	CY	Guam	GU
Czech Republic	CZ	Guatemala	GT
Denmark	DK	Guinea	GN
Djibouti	DJ	Guinea-Bissau	GW
Dominica	DM	Guyana	GY
Dominican Republic	DO	Haiti	HT
East Timor	TP	Honduras	HN
Ecuador	EC	Hong Kong	HK
Egypt	EG	Hungary	HU
El Salvador	SV	Iceland	IS
Equatorial Guinea	GQ	India	IN
Eritrea	ER	Indonesia	ID
Estonia	EE	Iran	IR
Ethiopia	ET	Iraq	IQ
Falkland Islands (Malvinas)	FK	Ireland	IE
Faroe Islands	FO	Israel	IL
Fiji	FJ	Italy	IT
Finland	FI	Jamaica	JM

Country	Abbreviation	Country	Abbreviation
Japan	JP	Moldova	MD
Jordan	JO	Monaco	MC
Kazakhstan	KZ	Mongolia	MN
Kenya	KE	Montserrat	MS
Kiribati	KI	Morocco	MA
Korea (North)	KP	Mozambique	MZ
Korea (South)	KR	Myanmar	MM
Kuwait	KW	Namibia	NA
Kyrgyzstan	KG	Nauru	NR
Laos	LA	Nepal	NP
Latvia	LV	Netherlands	NL
Lebanon	LE	Netherlands Antilles	AN
Lesotho	LS	New Caledonia	NC
Liberia	LR	New Zealand	NZ
Libya	LY	Nicaragua	NI
Liechtenstein	LI	Niger	NE
Lithuania	LT	Nigeria	NG
Luxembourg	LU	Niue	NU
Macau	MO	Norfolk Island	NF
Macedonia	MK	Northern Mariana Islands	MP
Madagascar	MG	Norway	NO
Malawi	MW	Oman	OM
Malaysia	MY	Pakistan	PK
Maldives	MV	Palau	PW
Mali	ML	Panama	PA
Malta	MT	Papua New Guinea	PG
Marshall Islands	MH	Paraguay	PY
Martinique	MQ	Peru	PE
Mauritania	MR	Philippines	PH
Mauritius	MU	Pitcairn	PN
Mayotte	YT	Poland	PL
Mexico	MX	Portugal	PT
Micronesia	FM	Puerto Rico	PR

Country	Abbreviation	Country	Abbreviation
Qatar	QA	Taiwan	TW
Romania	RO	Tajikistan	TJ
Russian Federation	RU	Tanzania	TZ
Rwanda	RW	Thailand	TH
Saint Kitts and Nevis	KN	Togo	TG
Saint Lucia	LC	Tokelau	TK
Saint Vincent		Tonga	TO
and The Grenadines	VC	Trinidad and Tobago	TT
Samoa	WS	Tunisia	TN
San Marino	SM	Turkey	TR
Sao Tome and Principe	ST	Turkmenistan	TM
Saudi Arabia	SA	Turks and Caicos Islands	TC
Senegal	SN	Tuvalu	TV
Seychelles	SC	Uganda	UG
Sierra Leone	SL	Ukraine	UA
Singapore	SG	United Arab Emirates	AE
Slovak Republic	SK	Uruguay	UY
Slovenia	SI	Uzbekistan	UZ
Solomon Islands	SB	Vanuatu	VU
Somalia	SO	Vatican City State	
South Africa	ZA	(Holy See)	VA
S. Georgia		Venezuela	VE
and S. Sandwich Islands	GS	Viet Nam	VN
Spain	ES	Virgin Islands (British)	VG
Sri Lanka	LK	Virgin Islands (U.S.)	VI
St. Helena	SH	Wallis and Futuna Islands	WF
Sudan	SD	Western Sahara	EH
Suriname	SR	Yemen	YE
Svalbard	SJ	Yugoslavia	YU
Swaziland	SZ	Zaire	ZR
Sweden	SE	Zambia	ZM
Switzerland	CH	Zimbabwe	ZW
Syria	SY		

Appendix B

Fine-Tuning Your Spell Checker

The basics of spell checking are covered in detail in Chapter 4. You can fine-tune your spell checker to make it behave the way you want it to. Below are buttons that appear in each of the spell checker's screens when a spell check is in progress.

The Other Spell Checker Buttons

Netscape	AOL	Internet Explorer/ Outlook Express	Purpose
Replace	Replace	Change	Replace the highlighted misspelled word with the suggested change.
Replace All	Replace All	Change All	Replace all occurrences of the misspelled word with the suggested change. If you consistently misspell a word in an e-mail, use this button to prevent the spell checker from stopping each time it encounters the misspelled word.
Check			If you don't know how to spell a word, you can type it in the **Word** field in the spell checker and click **Check** to see if it is spelled correctly.

Netscape	AOL	Internet Explorer/ Outlook Express	Purpose
Ignore	Skip	Ignore	Ignore this word, even though it is not in the dictionary. You might use this, for example, for an e-mail recipient's name that you use in your message.
Ignore All	Skip All	Ignore All	Ignore this word whenever it appears in the e-mail.
Learn	Learn	Add	Add the highlighted word to your custom dictionary. Use this for words you commonly use but which are not in the dictionary (i.e., people's names, cities, or technical terms).
Edit Dictionary			Edit words you have added to the custom dictionary.
Stop	Cancel	Cancel	Stop the spell check.
Help			Access on-screen help information
		Undo Last	Reverse the last change you made.
		Options	Access a variety of spell check options so you can customize the spell checker the way you want.

If You Don't Want To Spell Check Every Message

Perhaps you don't want the spell checker to run each time you send an e-mail to someone. You do have the choice of turning the automatic spell check off, running it only when you choose to.

To disable the automatic spell checker in your e-mail program, refer to

"Spell Check Your Document," in Chapter 4 (page 47), where you learned how to turn on your automatic spell checker. Follow the same steps described there for your e-mail program, except *remove* the check mark activating the spell checker.

In Netscape, you can still spell check an individual message after you have typed it by clicking the **Spelling** button at the top of the **Netscape Composition** screen:

In Outlook Express, activate your spell checker on demand by clicking **Tools** on the main menu of the **New Message** screen and then clicking on **Spelling** on the menu that appears, as shown here:

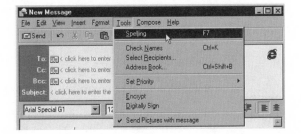

In AOL you can spell check an individual message clicking the **Spell Check** button on the toolbar of the **Write Mail** screen:

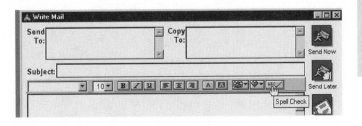

Tip

If you frequently run the spell checker manually, as describe here, you might want to remember the keyboard shortcut for activating this feature. You can spell check your outgoing e-mail at any time by pressing F7 located on the top row of your keyboard.

Tip

If your AOL automatic spell check is activated, you can override it and send an e-mail message without having it spell checked by holding down CTRL when you click the **Send Now** button.

Appendix C

E-mail Acronyms and Smileys

Now that e-mail is becoming so widely used, an entire vocabulary of abbreviations and emotion indicators, often called "smileys" or "emoticons" (for "emotion icons") has been created.

Are they silly? Yes. Do they serve a purpose? Again, yes. Since the communication medium is typed—not even handwritten—some of the nuances of communication using other techniques is lost. Smileys can be used to convey the implicit subtleties that might otherwise go unnoticed.

As you browse the Internet, especially in newsgroups and on mailing lists, you may well encounter these abbreviations and symbols. I've included a few of them here for your information.

Internet Abbreviations

24/7	24 hours a day, 7 days a week
A/S/L?	Age/sex/location?
BCNU	Be seein' you
BFN	Bye for now
<BG> or <bg>	Big grin
BRB	Be right back (as in "phone ringing—brb")
FAQ	Frequently asked question(s)
FWIW	For what it's worth
FYI	For your information
<g>	Grin
H & K	Hugs & kisses
HTTP	Hypertext transfer protocol

Internet Abbreviations

IC	I see
IDTT	I'll drink to that
IMAO	In my arrogant opinion
IMBO	In my biased opinion
IMCO	In my considered opinion
IMHO	In my humble opinion
KISS	Keep it simple stupid
LMAO	Laughing my a∗∗ off
LOL	Laughing out loud
LOL	Little old lady
LOM	Little old man
MYOB	Mind your own business
OBTW	Oh, by the way
OTOH	On the other hand
PEBKAC	Problem exists between keyboard and chair
PMJI	Pardon me for jumping in
QED	*Quod erat demonstrandum* or quite easily done
ROFL	Rolling on floor laughing
ROFLMAO	Rolling on floor laughing my a∗∗ off
SYSOP	System Operator
TIA	Thanks in advance
TTFN	Ta ta for now
URL	Uniform resource locator or universal resource locator

Emoticons/Smileys

(Turn your head sideways and use your imagination to see the expressions formed by the symbols below.)

:-) or :)	Smiling
:-(	Frowning
:-0	Surprise
8-0	Wow!—eyes wide with surprise
;-)	Winking/just kidding
:-x	My lips are sealed

Index